LIFE AFTER SCHOOL

by the same author

You Can Change the World
Everyday Teen Heroes Making a Difference Everywhere
Margaret Rooke
Forewords by Taylor Richardson and Katie Hodgetts
ISBN 978 1 78592 502 3
eISBN 978 1 78450 897 5

Meet the Dyslexia Club
The Amazing Talents, Skills and Everyday
Life of Children with Dyslexia
Margaret Rooke
Illustrated by Tim Stringer
Foreword by Róisín Lowe
ISBN 978 1 83997 843 2
eISBN 978 1 83997 844 9

Dyslexia Is My Superpower (Most of the Time)
Margaret Rooke
Forewords by Professor Catherine Drennan and Loyle Carner
ISBN 978 1 78592 299 2
eISBN 978 1 78450 606 3

Different Like Us!
Inspiring Real-Life Stories from Kids Everywhere
Margaret Rooke
Illustrated by Tim Stringer
ISBN 978 1 80501 292 4
eISBN 978 1 80501 294 8

LIFE AFTER SCHOOL

Dyslexic and Taking on the World!

Margaret Rooke

Jessica Kingsley Publishers
London and Philadelphia

First published in Great Britain by Jessica Kingsley Publishers
An imprint of John Murray Press

2

The fonts, layout and overall design of this book have been prepared according to dyslexia friendly principles. At JKP we aim to make our books' content accessible to as many readers as possible.

A CIP catalogue record for this title is available from the British Library and the Library of Congress

ISBN 978 1 80501 335 8
eISBN 978 1 80501 336 5

Printed and bound in the United States by Integrated Books International

Jessica Kingsley Publishers' policy is to use papers that are natural, renewable and recyclable products and made from wood grown in sustainable forests. The logging and manufacturing processes are expected to conform to the environmental regulations of the country of origin.

Jessica Kingsley Publishers
Carmelite House
50 Victoria Embankment
London EC4Y 0DZ

www.jkp.com

John Murray Press
Part of Hodder & Stoughton Ltd
An Hachette Company

The authorized representative in the EEA is Hachette Ireland,
8 Castlecourt Centre, Dublin 15, D15 XTP3, Ireland (email: info@hbgi.ie)

To L and H – great friends, and true role models for others finding their way

Contents

- Foreword by Marc Ingram 9
- A note about this book 13
- Introduction 15

Ch 1: You Can Always Change Your Mind 23

Joe, 24, Nottinghamshire, England 24

Leah, 21, London, England 30

Hayley, 26, South Lanarkshire, Scotland 38

Sarah, 20, Victoria, Australia 45

Henry, 20, County Dublin, Ireland 52

Jordan, 21, London, England 56

Ch 2: Follow Your Heart 65

Katelynn, 21, Michigan, USA 66

Will, 20, Victoria, Australia 71

Samuel, 19, Prince Edward Island, Canada 77

Anwen, 17, Carmarthen, Wales 84

Molly, 23, Stirlingshire, Scotland/York, England 92

Oliver, 23, Canterbury, England 101

Sarah, 18, Quebec, Canada 109

Ch 3: Take Your Time 115
Hannah, 26, London, England 116
Jamie, 21, Glasgow, Scotland 123
Ryan, 19, Kildare, Ireland 128
Rhomi, 26, London, England 133
Patrick, 24, Christchurch, New Zealand 139
George, 23, London, England 145

Ch 4: Find Ways to Help Yourself 151
Max, 24, Bay of Plenty, New Zealand 152
Zoe-Jane, 25, Birmingham, England 158
Po, 18, Victoria, Australia 166
Sam, 24, London, England 173
Gabriella, 24, East Lothian, Scotland 181
Rachel, 19, Oxford, England 187
Maleah, 19, Manchester, England 191

Ch 5: Never Look Back 197
Joe, 19, West Lothian, Scotland 198
Addison, 18, Ohio, USA 207
Eddie, 21, Leeds, England 214
Jenny, 26, Lagos, Nigeria 220
Jarred, 21, Aruba, the Caribbean/the Hague, the Netherlands 228
Helena, 24, London, England 232

Ch 6: How Dyslexia Helps Me Now 237
Evelyne, 25, County Wicklow, Ireland 238
Doug, 16, London, England 244
Lola, 26, London, England 250
Nick, 26, Bedford, England 256
Leah, 20, London, England 264
Elijah, 19, London, England 270

Ch 7: Giving Yourself the Best Chance to Succeed — 275

- Further Reading 284
- Further Help 285
- Acknowledgements 286
- With Thanks To 287

Foreword

At school I couldn't read or write, and I didn't want anyone around me to know.

I wasn't going to raise my hand and say, 'I can't do this work.' I was too ashamed. I couldn't do the basic things that a normal person could do. If I'd told a teacher privately, I knew someone would overhear. Instead, I argued with teachers and fought the other kids to get out of class and out of school. It worked, so I kept doing it.

After this I was put in a special class and that was better, but I left school at 15 with no qualifications. Nothing. All I'd heard for years was that we had to go to college and university to build a future. For me that was never going to be a thing. All I could see in front of me was a black hole.

At that time I believed I'd never have a job. I thought I would end up homeless. One night my friends were all online playing video games, and I remember being alone in my bedroom crying. My dream had always been to have my own house, my own family and my own business. None of this felt possible anymore.

I know my mum and my dad were worried for me. I'd heard my mum crying. They didn't know if I would do anything with my life. I had put myself down so much, I had ended up at a level where I felt worthless.

Then one day I talked to my careers adviser, and he told me about apprenticeships. After this, a thought came out of nowhere – I could be a butcher! It was just so random!

This may be because the only thing I was good at in school was when we learnt cookery. I'd loved that. I found out more about apprenticeships, and I became an apprentice with a craft butcher in a local farm shop.

On my first day I was so nervous. I thought if I said I was dyslexic they would get rid of me. When I told Frazer, who became my manager, I asked him, 'Will I lose my job?' and he laughed and said, 'Of course not. We will help you as much as you need.' From then on, I couldn't stop smiling. It felt like home.

People think butchers are 55-year-old men chopping up steaks, doing boring stuff. For me it's an amazing craft. It's about adding value. I think up different recipes, adding herbs and different flavours, working out all the new products I can come up with. My creative side has skyrocketed. Even my reading and writing are better, and while dyslexia doesn't go away, you learn to see the positives; the creativity, the passion and the confidence.

Now I'm 19, and I've been named Scotland's Apprentice of the Year. Something else – I have just bought my first house! I've also changed my health. I was morbidly obese. Now I've lost half my body weight through sessions in the gym and being careful what I eat. Some people don't recognise me.

If you're reading this, you may have similar worries to the ones I had. You may be anxious about your future. My message for you is to keep the one thing I didn't have, and that is hope. Remember you have your skills and determination. Keep these in mind and believe in yourself. Then work out which job or course will suit you, grab it and run with it. For a long time, I didn't believe in myself. Then I found the courage to build myself a future, to stop hiding my dyslexia. I stopped holding myself back. I became open to help from others.

For me apprenticeships have been the answer. You learn, you work, and you get paid a salary. Holy Moly! Your answer may be the same or it may be different but remember life after school can be so much better. A different world.

I found the path to make my life work. You can too. We're not alone. There are millions of us out there. Some have told their stories in this book, so take a look. They're all taking different journeys, and they all have ups and downs, but they show we can get there. We can all encourage each other to build a great future.

Marc Ingram
Dyslexia Scotland Young Ambassador

A note about this book

A while back I wrote the book *Dyslexia Is My Superpower (Most of the Time)*. This was a first. It gave more than 100 children and teenagers with dyslexia the chance to have their say. In it, they talk about their best qualities and the difficulties they face. They're clear about how schools can be improved and what teaching staff already do well. They know what could be done to help them succeed more. They all know what they are great at. For the first time, the true experts – the young people themselves – were having their say.

Nearly ten years after I first spoke to them, I've gone back to some of the children and teens in that book to see how their lives have turned out. I've added a few extra young people into the mix, and I've asked some of the original young dyslexic illustrators to express themselves in design once more.

This new book is a tribute to all those young dyslexic

minds, and to the young people all over the world I can't include. Everything in this book is a sign of the potential within these young people; of the skillsets that can propel them in the direction they want to go, even if they didn't find school easy, welcoming, or interesting, and even if their lessons didn't play to their strengths...

For young people with dyslexia everywhere, I hope those I've interviewed for this book will encourage you to look to your future with greater confidence. I hope you'll see that even if you take a wrong turn, there's always another chance. School may work out well for you or it may not, but afterwards there's a wide world of opportunities to grasp if you keep believing in yourself, find the goal you want to aim for, keep working hard, and surround yourself with people who are on your side.

Remember, you only have to be good at one thing to succeed. So gain support from others, follow your instincts, and be kind to yourself, acknowledging what you do well. Keep battling even when things feel tough. Keep having faith in who you are. When days in the classroom feel endless and exhausting, never forget that there truly is life after school.

@margsrooke

Introduction

If you:

- find yourself sitting in lessons you can't understand
- struggle to imagine a good future after years feeling stuck in the system
- compare yourself to others who look like they'll easily succeed
- face setbacks that feel out of your control

...this may be the book you're waiting for.

In these interviews, dyslexic young people explain how they've made their future work for them. They prove that you don't have to follow the crowd to do well. You too can create your own story and make the most of your life.

When you're dyslexic, it's hard not to compare yourself to those headed for the best exam results and top universities. It's all too easy to feel anxious when any hope of the future you want for yourself seems light years away.

This book is proof that there is life after school, no matter how hard you find the work you're given there. These teenagers and other young people I've talked to have looked for a brighter life after they leave. Whether they are now at college, university, or work, they are using their individual talents to help them thrive.

They explain what has helped them and what has blocked their way. If they find dyslexia causing them problems, they think about ways to overcome these. When their career path doesn't go the way they hoped, they stay open-minded, work hard, and discover another route.

You'll meet Hannah, from the UK, who's become a social worker with a first-class degree, years after failing all her exams at high school when she was 16. 'Someone should have told me I could achieve later in my life, but no one did', she told me.

You'll meet Samuel, from Canada, who uses his dyslexic talents in his job in construction, and Katelynn, from the USA, who's becoming a teacher to help other kids get the attention they need in class.

There's Sam, who used his visual strengths to study cell biology, and Rhomi, whose problems with hair loss have led to a business selling natural shampoo made to her own recipe.

Making the Most of School

Someone who's about to join them is Freddie, who's 17. He's in his last year of high school and is looking forward to life afterwards. In his words: 'I've never been the greatest fan of the education system.'

While he's still there, he's made the decision to do all he can to succeed. 'Realistically you might as well get what you can from it when you have to be there' is his advice. 'Then you have a better chance to do what you want when you leave.'

'If you face your lessons head on, rather than shy away from what you have to learn, you'll eventually see improvements.'

Freddie's also a believer in having the confidence to ask teachers for the support he needs. 'If you're already struggling, you want to help yourself do the best you can,' he says.

And if there are lessons you enjoy, throw yourself into them to help balance out your time in education. This can be hugely valuable as you build a picture of what you want in your life.

* * *

Tahirah Yasin, founder of www.theneurodirectory.co.uk, says she coped with high school, a particularly tough time, by having friends and teachers who understood her challenges and helped her keep going. She remembers learning, failing, and then learning again.

'I watched closely how others approached their studies and how they mixed with each other socially. By mirroring them, I used this as a chance to understand my weaknesses and work on them.'

Tahirah worked out that she needed to increase her confidence by celebrating her 'small wins'. She saw any minor achievement as a step forward. She replaced negative thoughts that came into her mind with positive ones. And she set herself small, manageable goals, giving herself a sense of progress.

We can all do this, remembering to celebrate anything we do well, from helping a friend who needs us, to remembering our sports kit if we usually forget it. We can set achievable targets, from keeping to homework deadlines to checking our work through rather than just handing it in.

Moving On

For the transition from school to college, university, or work, Tahirah suggests the following:

Communicate openly with your family and friends about how important this step is for you, to gain their support.

Be the best you can at being you. Don't try to mould yourself into someone else's idea of success. Your journey is your own.

Take note of what you've achieved and use this to keep reminding yourself about how much you've progressed.

Embrace opportunities to learn in every aspect of your life. Learning doesn't stop because you've left school.

Trust your instincts and believe that everything will work out. Your journey is unique, and your path will unfold in its own time.

Find yourself a mentor who can help you with big decisions, and help you recognize your strengths.

Push yourself forwards, even when things are tough and changes are challenging.

Tahirah acknowledges that if you're from a minority background or have additional issues or needs, difficulties can feel magnified. 'Seek support when needed', she stresses. 'Surround yourself with people who understand your challenges and respect your experiences. In the end, for me, dyslexia was never something to hold me back, only a thing I knew I had.'

Some teenagers leave school and see a world of choices ahead of them, in the many thousands of directions a school leaver can take. If you don't have that level of confidence, this is a good time to think seriously about your future. Maybe the young people in this book can inspire you.

Some went to college or university and found it easier than everything that came before. Some went to college, regretted it, and changed direction. Some started work straight from high school, then went to university when they were older. Some went straight out to work when they finished high school and never looked back.

Many were inspired in their choice of work by following the interests they had developed outside school from a very early age. Learning takes place everywhere, at every stage of our lives, not just inside the school gates.

Your Problem-Solving Skills Can Guide You

College student advisor Barbara Reissner explains that for those who have faced barriers, including dyslexia, the path to the future they want may not be straightforward. They may sometimes need to take a more complex route. This is where their ability to think in different and creative ways can be a vital strength.

'Use your problem-solving skills and your capacity to assert yourself to get to where you want', she says. 'Many young people in this book do this. They find a different path. Experience gained outside academic study, in voluntary work, part-time jobs, and travel can all help you to achieve your goals.'

And none of us should ever forget the work from the Dyslexic Advantage group in the USA. Their research is clear. Successful adults with dyslexia say their achievements have come largely from focusing on their strengths, not making good what they find difficult, though this has its place too. Look for where your skills and qualities lie – in maths, in friendship, in design, in empathy, in clear communications, in any other direction. Think about how these assets can help you find a future that works for you.

'For many with dyslexia, life seems to begin once they step outside of school and begin to discover their talents, strengths, and the creative vision they bring to the outside world', says Fernette Eide of Dyslexic Advantage. 'It is the real world that is their canvas.'

CHAPTER 1

You Can Always Change Your Mind

JARRED DE VRIES @TRTWTATTOOo2

JOE, 24, NOTTINGHAMSHIRE, ENGLAND

> **"My story shows that it's not always the best idea to rush to university. You're better off waiting to check what you want to do. Invest your time that way. Don't let schools push you into making the choices they think are right for you."**

With a first-class degree in commercial photography, you might expect me to be working as a photographer. You'd be wrong!

I'm a farmer, and I love it – and I didn't even consider farming when I left school.

My story shows that it's not always the best idea to rush to university. You're better off waiting to check what you want to do. Invest your time that way. Certainly, don't let schools push you into making the choices they think are right for you.

Primary school was a struggle for me. Mum has helped me over the years, but one big thing was that during primary she homeschooled me for one day a week. This stopped life feeling so exhausting and relentless and helped me pick up some of the foundations, like getting through reading.

I think the most important thing anyone with dyslexia needs is time to understand something. We don't need people to get frustrated with us, so this worked well.

At secondary school, I liked sciences, but I didn't like English at all. They didn't ever seem to get me in the right set. At the start they put me in the top sets, but I struggled in English, and nothing seemed to make any difference. Then they put me into the bottom set, I also felt I didn't belong there as the pace was too slow, but they left me there for the rest of my time at school.

Whenever I had the chance, I was careful to choose practical subjects like engineering and art, and PE felt good for my mental health, but it was a relief to end school.

The ending was strange to say the least. I had extra time for the exams because I am dyslexic, so I walked out after this and that was it. Everybody else had left. I found myself walking out of an empty school. Maybe in one way this meant that I never looked back.

After this, I went to post-16 college and did maths, physics, and photography, but I struggled with the maths and dropped out. I stuck with physics, but it was photography that kept me going.

Thanks to my A Level* portfolio of photos, I was given an unconditional offer at university and I accepted this and decided to start the next term.

During the first year I was still thinking I could make a go of photography. I really enjoyed it. We learnt everything including processing the films. Then, that summer, a

* A Levels are exams taken in most of the UK at 18

family friend asked me to photograph a wedding for them. I agreed, but I found it incredibly stressful and thought this career wasn't for me.

Good Grades

I carried on into my second year, even though I had doubts. I was getting good grades and wanted to see if I could think of another gap in the market for taking photos. By the third year, I had lost my dad, and I was going through a lot of grief. I was thinking it wasn't the right time to be doing this degree. Again, I stuck at it, and they awarded me a first. I think they could see how I put my heart and soul into my work.

With losing my dad, I didn't want to have time to think about anything. I just wanted to go out to work and take my mind off things. So I started working in a local bar, pulling pints. This was a great decision partly because it was where I met my now fiancée. It was also great because I found out the guy I was working with was doing a bit of potato grading for a local farm during the day and needed some help. I thought I could work on the farm during the day and work in the pub at night. That would fill my time.

I've been at the farm ever since. It's been three years, and I've worked my way up. I'm now driving the potato harvester, and they've put me through spraying qualifications, chainsaw tests, forklift truck qualifications – any courses I want to take, they let me do.

My love of farms wasn't out of the blue. When I was younger, there was a sheep farm next door. I used to go and help feed the lambs before and after primary school. I loved it. The best part of my day.

I carried on helping when I went to secondary school.

Ever since, I've been into farming. I often went to tractor shows to look at the tractors and watch ploughing competitions. I loved the outdoors lifestyle. Today I went out of the house at six in the morning and I haven't been inside yet and it's the end of the day. Even at weekends, I can't stand being inside.

Another thing I love about the farm is that it gives me a lot of time on my own. It gives me time for reflection, and I need that.

The work plays to my dyslexic strengths. I always scare my mum if I'm driving her somewhere because my spatial awareness is so sharp. I know how big a vehicle is and what it can fit through. She gets terrified if I'm driving her in the car. She thinks I'm about to scratch the sides. I tell her, 'You could fit a tractor through here.'

My mind is good at problem solving and thinking things through. With farming there's always something to fix. I spend a lot of time in the winter welding and making good everything we broke during the summer.

I can't say I regret doing my degree. I really enjoyed it. I spend some of my time now taking wildlife photos for the pleasure of it, but I also want to put together a portfolio: 'Nature from the cab of a tractor', that kind of thing. University helped my reading, and I learnt how to skim through things, but I still do struggle especially with blocks of text. The words all move around, and I have no chance. I find the long names of chemical sprays we use difficult. I take my time to make sure I'm not picking up the wrong can. I always doubt myself and double check.

Some things I learnt in school help me. The physics side of maths is good for problem solving, but mostly the way I learn is through dealing with everyday problems at work.

I work very hard, and that's my main recommendation for anyone with dyslexia. You have to work hard to bring success in life. Follow your gut. Your instincts about whether a job is right or wrong for you will be correct. If something doesn't feel right, it probably isn't.

Good friends are vital as well, to talk things through with and help you solve problems. I especially like having friends from different age groups with all the different experience they have.

My friends have to put up with me misspelling text messages, but they understand what I mean. When it comes to social media, I mainly post photographs and don't tend to write.

One stumbling block I have is my short-term memory. If my fiancée says 'Can you do this and this and this?' I have no chance of remembering everything. She has to tell me the first couple of things and text me the rest.

I tell her we haven't had some conversations and then she reminds me about them, and I admit she is right.

School is only a short time, when everything seems to be about exam things. It's hoops you've got to jump through, trying to find bits you enjoy, while getting to the next part of life which should be a lot more fun. I'm so pleased to be where I am now, doing something I love. If you can do that, as the old saying goes, you won't have to work a day in your life.

> "I work very hard, and that's my main recommendation for anyone with dyslexia. You have to work hard to bring success in life. And follow your gut. Your instincts about whether a job is right or wrong for you will be correct. If something doesn't feel right, it probably isn't."

LEAH, 21, LONDON, ENGLAND

"The moment I left school I couldn't have been happier. My life became my own. At the same time, everything seemed daunting. I knew I could lie at home all day and do nothing. Or I could get up, go ahead, and chase my dreams."

Life after school is like a rollercoaster ride. I don't think anyone prepares you for those ups and downs, and what a massive responsibility every decision is. Maybe nothing could have helped me, but some guidance from school might have been useful. Instead, you're just left on your own.

From having a structure to your days, suddenly you have to find your feet. When it comes to friendships, everyone is on their own path, so you have to make full-on arrangements to meet people. You've got to make your own decisions about your future and choose how your life will go.

The moment I left school I couldn't have been happier. I was relieved. There's no other word to express how I felt. My life became my own. At the same time, everything seemed daunting. I knew I could lie at home all day and do nothing. Or I could get up, go ahead, and actually chase my dreams.

Doors Were Shut

My dream had always been to be a nurse for children who were seriously ill or dying – a paediatric palliative care nurse. I had always wanted to give back to society in that way. My problem was that wherever I applied, I found that the door was shut to me because I hadn't passed my maths GCSE.* I tried every course I could find, university courses, foundation courses, everything, and they all said they wouldn't take me as I wasn't qualified. I had other qualifications but not the one they wanted.

This was a huge blow, leaving me stranded with nothing. I had no idea where to go. I felt I had so much to give and nowhere to give it to.

I started a nannying job that was bittersweet. I got along with the family well, unless I tried to stand up for myself about anything. Then I couldn't find the right words.

I moved on to work at a children's nursery. This has been good for me. I've just taken my Level 3 Early Years Diploma, equivalent to A Levels.** The best news is that I've also found something I want to do more than be a children's nurse and that's to work in play therapy for children in hospices who are seriously ill and dying. I can start that course when I've worked in early years for two years.

* GCSEs are qualifications taken in most of the UK at 16

** A Levels are qualifications taken in most of the UK at 18

* * *

At school I felt that there wasn't enough support, but one of our teachers empowered us more than the others. She told us that just because we were in the bottom set, it didn't mean we couldn't get to the same place as someone who was higher up. It might take longer but we could still get there and be just as successful.

She showed us this movie called *Coach Carter*, based on a true story, about these boys in America who were playing basketball, and most of them were going to end up in jail. Their coach wouldn't allow them to play until they'd started going to classes and getting results. The movie has the biggest place in my heart. It is so empowering to hear that you can achieve what you want to. You can rise above the limitations other people place on you.

I had some humiliating times at school. Sometimes I think they've affected me in a bad way, but sometimes I think they've pushed me forwards. I'd love to go back to school and say, 'I've actually made something of myself'. I sensed some of my teachers didn't have any faith that I would.

I don't honestly think my years at school helped me with my life now at all. I learnt to read on my own, at my own pace, though my reading has gone downhill since then. I had to teach myself to type. I couldn't tell anyone I was dyslexic in those days. It was a massive problem for me. Now I'm so open, I will say it from the get-go.

I don't think school teaches us the right things, like how to save money, how to budget, and what our credit scores are. We need to know what togs mean on a duvet. I have no idea. Some of these seem like small things but we need to know.

When I left, I couldn't face taking my GCSE maths again, but I'm taking the maths in my current course which is easier – it's for people like me who just can't pass. I haven't been to the classes because they would put me under too much pressure. I prefer to struggle on my own.

Most of what I've learnt has come from where I'm working now. I learn about how to look after small children from my colleagues and I learn so much from the children. I look up to my line manager. She believes in me more than anyone. I think she just sees something special in me, a lot of potential.

When I first started there, I used to ask everyone, 'When will I be confident like you?' I used to look at them and wonder when I wouldn't be anxious when I was speaking to the parents. Now I am that confident.

One problem I have is after nappy changing. We always need to write down when we've changed a child. This is because if a parent says, 'They came home with a poo', we can take a look and say, 'This is when we changed them'. The trouble is I always forget to write it down, even though people remind me. I think genuinely my dyslexic brain just goes off somewhere. I get distracted and the thought goes straight out of my head.

Terrible Timekeeping

I'm good at timekeeping with work, but not outside of work. One of my friends always gets somewhere way early. Then she's there waiting for my text saying, 'I'm going to be late', or 'Can we move it to this time?' I do think I've gotten better as I've gotten older. Sometimes she says, 'Wow, you're actually here on time', but I know she used to get annoyed with me.

My texting is terrible. I reply in my head, and I do believe that I've replied. A couple of hours later I go back and look and I'm like, 'I didn't even send that text'. I think about it, and then it just flows out of my head. That can be a bit of a problem.

One way dyslexia has helped my friendships is that I'm a supportive person. I've learnt a lot about compassion because of everything I experienced at the schools I went to and how well I remember every kindness that came my way afterwards.

Relationships can have difficulties. I was talking to someone who said, 'You didn't even listen to anything I just said'. I told him, 'I think you forget that I'm dyslexic. It may seem like everything's fine because I can speak and listen and read and write, but there is a difference with my brain'. He asked me what I meant, and I said, 'Listen mate, by the time you've got to the end of what you're saying, I'm still trying to process what you said at the start'.

I had to explain that although you can't physically see the difference, it is there, and it's hidden. I had to reassure him I wasn't ignoring him, I just needed time to work everything out.

Dyslexia is helpful in other ways. I use a lot of creativity at work. We have sessions that we call bucket time, when you show things to the children, and I've made sure it's interactive. This means the children get to feel things that appeal to all their senses, like smell, hearing, taste, visuals. I ask the children what differences they notice, maybe one surface will be prickly, and one will be smooth, and we discuss this. It makes things exciting for them. Rather than just asking them what colour something is, I'll say, 'Close your eyes and see what this makes you think of'.

Help from Others

The biggest benefit I've had is a supportive mum. I've learnt loads from my line manager too. They both have only wanted the best for me.

We all need that level of understanding, so if you are trying to support a loved one with dyslexia I think that's the most important thing to remember. Be gentle because dyslexia isn't the easiest thing, and take things slow. Reassure them that the future will be bright if they find what they're good at and work hard. Don't get annoyed at the small things, like when we lose our focus or interest.

Sometimes I think about my friends who went to university and that they've graduated so they are the successful ones, but then they see me as someone who has a job. We all need to believe in who we are.

All of us with dyslexia need to have faith in ourselves. If we don't succeed at something at the first opportunity, we must keep on trying. I was devastated when I didn't get to do nursing, but I've learnt that when one door closes another one opens. I thought everything was crashing down, but now I'm happy that happened.

KERI BAKER

I've always told myself that I'm never going to be able to change the world, but I can make a big impact on people's lives. The caring and compassionate side of me wants to help with the worst situations people go through and try to make things as good as they can be. As I said, I want to give back.

> **"Sometimes I think about my friends who went to university and that they've graduated so they are the successful ones, but then they see me as someone who has a job. We all need to believe in who we are."**

HAYLEY, 26, SOUTH LANARKSHIRE, SCOTLAND

"In this job I've learnt so much about where gold comes from, where diamonds come from, the quality of the diamonds, the clarity. I've learnt about the way stones are graded, the different cuts. When someone's looking at a diamond ring, I need to be able to tell them everything about it."

High school wasn't the best time for me. I felt like a bit of a loner when I was there and was relieved when I left. College was where I recreated myself. I decided on the first day I wasn't going to be the same as I used to be. I was no longer going to feel ashamed about dyslexia and I wasn't going to be shy or let people walk all over me. I met good people there and I'm still close to a lot of them now.

At college I started acting as if I was confident. Inside my head I was going, 'Hayley, you can't keep pretending like this', but after two years I wasn't pretending anymore. I didn't take criticism from people if it wasn't reasonable. I was everything I wanted to be, comfortable and secure in myself and my abilities.

This was when I became open about my dyslexia. Sometimes people don't quite understand that some things are difficult for me because I'm dyslexic, so these days I tell them straight off the bat. It's clear now that it's so much better for me to make people aware.

I had difficult times because I was studying journalism and I struggled with a lot of writing and spelling, but they did give me support. I ended up falling out of love with the course because it didn't feel creative. The writing was very specific and regimented. This was heartbreaking and took me some time to come to terms with because I had always wanted to be a journalist.

I still write short stories and a blog. My letters can get mixed up and I can make a lot of mistakes, but I still love writing.

One thing dyslexia doesn't affect is my reading. I can completely disappear into a book, especially when I can identify with a character. The first book I ever read was in the first year of high school. It was called *Everything Beautiful* by Simmone Howell. It's about an overweight girl who is sent to a Christian summer camp by her parents because she's getting into trouble, but she has her own mindset. She decides to go with her tiniest clothes. She's just being herself. I always wanted to be like her, and I gained a lot of confidence from the book. I still read it to this day, if there's something in my life I can't handle and I want to feel more powerful.

When I walked away from journalism, I had to decide what to do. I knew I was good with the public, so I worked in a local pharmacy. This felt great, though it had challenges. Dealing with the long, complicated names of prescription drugs was a big adjustment, especially because you felt you had somebody's life in your hands. Even though there was a pharmacist to check what you were doing – and there are lots of checks – you're the initial person to put this person's medication together and that's what's at the back of your head.

I double-checked and triple-checked everything. It took me a long time to feel comfortable in the job, but when I did, it came easily. This was one of the first times when I've done something that should have been difficult, and I didn't find it difficult.

Through the Covid lockdowns, we were one of the only places that were open, and customers were getting angry and upset, wanting us to prescribe things we weren't allowed to prescribe and taking it out on us. We told them they needed to get prescriptions from their doctors, and they would go, 'It's on you if I die'. I was like, 'Excuse me?' It was a small chemist in a rundown area. They saw me as a young girl without stopping to think that I was someone trained for this job. They'd even say, 'I want to speak to a man'.

A Sparkling New Job

After this I felt I needed to work at something more enjoyable. I wanted to be happier. I left and did some call centre work which did not suit me, and then nearly two years ago I started working for Beaverbrooks, the jewellers.

This is the best move I've ever made. It feels like everything has fallen into place. I'm in the store dealing with customers every day, selling diamonds, jewellery, and watches. Everyone is much happier here. Who can be unhappy around jewellery?

Of course, we spend a lot of time handling expensive items and so the company has to have a lot of trust in you, which feels good.

I think the job is great for me because I'm an understanding person. If someone comes in looking for an engagement ring, they may not have much money. They may not be able to afford the biggest diamond. I try to help them see that an engagement ring is a symbol of your love for someone. A less expensive ring doesn't mean you love someone less. It's not about the size of the stone, it's about the promise you make. I explain that whatever they give their partner will be beautiful to them. I'm an open person and quite emotional and that comes over.

We make sure our customers feel comfortable with us. They sit down and have a coffee or tea or Prosecco, whether they're buying a £17,000 ring or a £20 pair of earrings. We know that £20 can be a lot of money for some people.

If someone comes back to buy something else, I remember them. I ask them how the necklace went down or how the ring went down. When they say, 'Do you remember that?', of course that makes me feel better than I have in my whole life! I'm doing something interesting. I'm looking at beautiful jewellery all day and my customers are at peace and relaxed. This means they open up to you. One woman whose husband was dying said he'd told her to come into the store and buy a particular bracelet. He'd seen it on our website, and he wanted to buy it for her. This work fills my heart and makes me think the world is good.

In this job I've learnt so much about the making of jewellery: where gold comes from, where diamonds come from, the quality of the diamonds, the clarity. It's very technical. I've learnt about the way stones are graded, the different cuts. When someone's looking at a diamond ring, I need to be able to tell them everything about it.

Top Tip from Hayley: I think this kind of learning comes more easily to me because it's visual. I'm doing a jewellery qualification at the moment, so I do need textbooks to help with that, but I'm a visual person, so I make my notes colour co-ordinated as it's the best way for me to learn.

I would probably say the way I've done most of my learning is through life experience. I don't think school did much for me. I enjoyed college for the most part, but I have learnt more in the last two or three years than I have in my entire life.

Buying My Own Home

Thanks to my work, I've been able to buy my flat which was probably one of the biggest challenges of my life so far: taking on the responsibilities; taking on a mortgage; taking on bills and having a budget. I found this difficult. My head got so foggy with the pressure. The world seemed to be running past me, moving at 100 miles an hour. It took me a long time to edge into it and to be comfortable with the paperwork. I'm in a good position now and I'm still learning every day.

It was important for me to buy my own house, and I think about running my own business one day. I had always wanted to be very academic, but something inside me said no. I just need to live my life.

A lot of people at work think dyslexia helps me solve problems that come up there. Some things are difficult for me, but some things are difficult for other people, and I can deal with them well. If there's a discrepancy in our stock, I'm the one who can figure out what happened and make sure everything is correct. I love getting my teeth into a problem.

I advise anyone with dyslexia to understand themselves: what they're good at and what their difficulties are. Then you can do things your way and get the same results.

Dyslexia affects me in my relationship with my boyfriend. If I feel overwhelmed at the end of the day with everything I have to deal with, I need to sit in silence. He used to take this personally and think I was annoyed at him. Now he knows this is how I deal with stuff.

Lots of other people support me too, including my family. If you're supporting someone with dyslexia, the best thing you can do is give them time. Be patient. They may not yet know what they need, but when they find this out, you can be there for them.

If you're struggling with dyslexia right now, just remember there are people all over the world with the same struggle. Just take the time for yourself. Figure out what works for you and what you care about. Don't be scared of what other people think. Many of them will have similar difficulties. Try reading *Dyslexia Is My Superpower (Most of the Time)*. My story's in that book. I read the stories from the other children and teenagers in there, and they make me feel so much better. Even looking at the front cover makes me think, 'This is full of people with dyslexia. It's not just me'.

This book will be the same. We're not alone.

"I advise anyone with dyslexia to understand themselves: what they're good at and what their difficulties are. Then you can do things your way and get the same results."

SARAH, 20, VICTORIA, AUSTRALIA

> **"Most of my learning has happened outside of school, just by watching what's going on around me. While the things you learn in school are great, I think some of the things you learn outside of school are way more important."**

The most important thing any of us can do is to believe in ourselves. We have to be our own biggest supporter. If we believe we can do what we want, we can push ourselves to achieve this. Life can work out even if it's in a complicated, backwards way.

I didn't believe until the end of high school that I could maybe do something really cool with my life. For a very long time I thought I would be stuck somewhere because I could only achieve so much. In the end, I found a passion that I loved, and I let that take me where it was going to take me. It has given me this life.

Coming out of school, I was ready to leave. I thought I wanted to do engineering. It's an idea that's always sort of been there, because drawing and seeing things visually has always been a strength of mine. So I did a gap year working in engineering and architecture. The people I worked with were great and the things I learnt were awesome.

Despite this, I missed the personal connections I thought I'd find in other work. I realized that working within the team was when I was having the most fun and making the biggest impact. I wanted to have more contact with others; to be able to help people and see their progress.

A Rollercoaster Ride

Since then, life has been a rollercoaster ride. I realized that uni will always be there, and until I go, I wanted to do awesome things.

One awesome thing I do is that I mentor young women in the Vanuatu Islands, teaching them about safe sex and health care. I love this volunteering, and it has helped me see the future I want.

My plan is to be a regional nurse in Northern Australia, working in remote places. I want to spend a lot of time on the road, getting to know communities and what they need. Then I'd love to be able to travel while I'm nursing. I like the idea that nursing can be more than working in a hospital – my brain works like this, shooting in different directions.

Travelling has already been a big part of my life. In Year 9, when I was 14, I had the opportunity through school to go to Nepal. We did a week working at a school there, and a three-week trek that included hiking to Ama Dablam, the next biggest base camp to Mount Everest, which was incredible.

The next year I had another amazing opportunity. I did a full year youth exchange in Switzerland, while a Swiss girl came to live in my part of Australia. I lived over there with host families and had the chance to travel to 15 other European countries.

In Switzerland, I learnt Swiss German, the language they spoke where I was staying. I had tried to learn German in school when I was younger and struggled. Within three months of being in Switzerland I could understand conversations and was having my own. After six months I felt I understood everything going on around me. I attended classes and took exams. It was being there and hearing it all the time that makes the difference.

Coming home able to speak another language made me realize how much I could achieve. I found a confidence within myself and came out of my shell. I knew I could be caring and open-minded, and now I realized I could push myself into doing things that made me feel uncomfortable but that I could gain from.

I wanted to keep on seeing the world, so I've done a lot of travel since school, earning money to pay for it. I was working as a skiing instructor until recently when I tore a ligament in my knee, so I've had to come home and have surgery. I'll stay here to let my knee recover, and then I'll go to university to do nursing in March.

Someone who influenced me is one of the nurses who works with the ski instructors. She told me that the job can take you to wherever you want it to. I want to grow in it and change it and see where it takes me next.

I also realized that the opportunities in front of me were

far greater than I thought. Going to Nepal, doing the exchange, and everything I've done since, all just built on each other and showed me what I could do and what else is out there.

> **Top Tip from Sarah:** When I was younger, I spent so much time pushing myself and worrying about keeping up with everyone else, instead of thinking about what I wanted. When I was older, I found my strengths and made the decision to choose subjects that I loved and enjoyed doing, like arts and sport.

When I was at school, I had to learn how to deal with some of the things I found difficult and find strategies that worked. I had to spend longer studying and trying to understand what everybody else was understanding so much more easily.

Ultimately, I think working so hard became a strength and I surprised myself with my end of Year 12 results. I showed myself that I'm capable if I just believe in myself. For a long time, I didn't feel like that. A lot of credit goes to my mum. She did all the research and figured out what I needed to be doing to be able to do my best.

I think through school I learnt how even though being dyslexic has its challenges, it can also be, like Mum would call it, a superpower that has given me so much. It has made me feel brave and special. I see the world in pictures and have a different way of thinking about

things. I know how important it is to work hard because I've always had to.

On my year overseas, I learnt how to be brave and confident, and I know these are important skills to take into my future.

Facing Difficulties

Sometimes I have faced difficulties, like when I'm working out how to apply for visas. Doing research online can be hard too, but I no longer feel like I'm falling behind or not learning as much as I should be.

Top Tip from Sarah: I've found that listening helps me take things in much more easily. Now I have all these apps on my phone so I can listen to documents instead of reading them. Then I can process what I need to know faster and understand what's going on. I use these every day.

Thanks to this, I feel dyslexia has only benefited me, and though my spelling is horrific, I don't have any shame. It may have held me back in my friendships when I was younger, but not anymore.

Supporting someone with dyslexia is as simple as being there for them, and just learning what dyslexia means and how you can help. Tell them they're fully capable of doing whatever they want.

My advice for anyone's future is not just to jump into something. Find your strengths and figure out what you want to do. Life is much better after school. I've had opportunities to do so many incredible things. Just because no one around me is doing what I'm doing doesn't mean I can't. It makes me feel more motivated.

Dyslexia has brought me the confidence to do things I love that would have scared me previously. We can do this when we have the right support and we believe in ourselves.

> **"Most of my learning has happened outside of school, just by watching what's going on around me. While the things you learn in school are great, I think some of the things you learn outside of school are way more important. On my year overseas, I learnt how to be brave and confident, and I know these are important skills to take into my future."**

DAISY BATES

'The lightning bolt of a new thought crashing out of my brain, right through my skull and into reality.'

HENRY, 20, COUNTY DUBLIN, IRELAND

> **"I was doing a lot of manual labour, and I came to think I was more suited to using my creativity. I wanted to use that part of my brain."**

When I left school I was disappointed with my results as my maths grade didn't meet the standard for the engineering course I wanted to take. I had tried as hard as I could and fell one mark shy.

As a result of my maths, after leaving school I worked for two years as an apprentice fitter, welding for an engineering company. The work suited me. I was pleased to have a job I enjoyed and made money in, that enabled me to have more freedom and buy a sports car!

I was doing a lot of manual labour, and I came to think I was more suited to working with ideas where I could use my creativity. I thought that if I worked as an engineer, I wouldn't be given free rein, but I would be able to use that part of my brain.

Retaking My Maths

I was apprehensive about making the change at first because I was settled in what I was doing, but it was the right decision.

The course I was applying for at uni had its own maths

exam that I had to pass. I studied very hard and luckily I did well, and I was given a place. I had learnt a lot from my time doing the apprenticeship, but I am so glad that I had the courage to follow my dreams.

Now I'm at university. I've worked on a few projects during this first year and my ideas have gone down well. I've won two out of the three engineering competitions and I'm delighted with that.

Top Tip from Henry: Studying at school had always been difficult for me, but I put my own systems in place to help me deal with this. I created my own study techniques, making cards to help myself, writing everything down and talking to myself about what I was learning. I'd created a process of reading, getting what I'd read down on paper and then getting it into my head. This seemed to work for me.

I use the same techniques now as this suits the way my mind works. This has helped more than anything school taught – I've taught myself how to learn. I think that's part of the problem-solving aspect of the way I think, and it's been very, very helpful. It motivates me to achieve well.

Luckily in this engineering course we've only had one essay to write this year. This meant I didn't have to do much writing and I'm happy with that. I quite liked English at school, but I could never structure an essay and they took me so long. This was quite frustrating because I am interested in concepts, but putting them onto paper in a concise way was difficult.

My advice to anyone trying to succeed with dyslexia is don't take on a problem as one huge step but break it down and pick it apart. I think that's all you need to do to get from A to B. Think things through before you act on them.

Dyslexia still affects me. I find texting is hard, trying to get what I want to say across. It's easier now I'm in college because I can see people and talk to them, not text all the time.

My mother and my brother support me the most. My brother isn't dyslexic, so I learn from his different way of looking at things. If you want to support someone with dyslexia, listening to them is important, rather than trying to force ideas onto them. Let them speak. I guess we get enough forced onto us that doesn't come naturally.

I think working is easier than school life. There's a lot less sitting down. In terms of manual work, I found a lot of people who went to work straight from school had dyslexia or other learning difficulties, and they were good workers. It might be different in a field like office work. It's so important to follow your strengths.

When you leave school you have the freedom to make choices that suit your abilities. You have more power than you had in school, when life was very restrictive.

I'm positive about my future. I'm hoping to concentrate on mechanical engineering next year, then graduate and go into a field to use the skills I have. I know I've made the right choice.

> "My advice to anyone trying to succeed with dyslexia is don't take on a problem as one huge step but break it down and pick it apart. I think that's all you need to do to get from A to B. Think things through before you act on them."

JORDAN, 21, LONDON, ENGLAND

"There's a connection between my design skills, my ability to problem solve, and my dyslexia. My job allows me to help people, and I build new relationships every day. I never know what a day is going to throw at me, so I'm kept on my toes."

Life has taken me somewhere I didn't expect to be, to a job I wasn't expecting, but I don't regret any of it.

When I was younger, I had a lot of support with dyslexia and followed the pretty standard route from school to college and then straight to university where I studied interior design.

At university I discovered I had a big passion for design. I had always had an interest, but I wasn't quite sure until then how much I loved it.

I learnt that interior design was not what I expected. I thought it would be colourful and kind of 'free', but once I started the course, I realized that it's about problem solving. It's strategic. It involves working with many different people, including architects, engineers, and builders, and it's so much more complex than I had thought. I liked this more than the 'softer side' I was expecting. I enjoyed the site visits and working on practical solutions to technical problems.

After university there was so much competition for

design jobs, and I didn't manage to get one. Then a job came up with a housing association, and for the last six months I've been a housing officer, managing tenancies, organizing repairs and rent collection, and working on customer relations. This means I take on all landlord responsibilities for the 200 properties I manage.

I use some of the elements of my degree in the work that I do. My studying has meant I have a better understanding of buildings and structures, so that helps a lot with repairs.

I think there's a level of connection between my design skills, my ability to problem solve, and my dyslexia. I miss designing, but I really like this job. It allows me to help people, and I build new relationships every day. There is so much to do. I never know what a day is going to throw at me, so I'm kept on my toes. The job has broadened me as a person. I didn't realize the toll that finances and housing difficulties place on some people's lives. I have a much greater understanding of that now, and much more appreciation for my life and everything my family has.

Keeping an Open Mind

So design was one passion, and now I have another in the form of improving social housing. I've always been open to what comes my way. While I'd still like to design, I'm now thinking of designing for everyday places – for schools, young people, and housing associations. This job has shown me how broad design is and how much opportunity there is. Working on high-end homes is great, but it's also good to have the satisfaction that you are helping someone and making a change in their life.

When I was at school, I had no idea that life would turn out this well. I struggled with dyslexia and spent six years seeing a tutor, Delia. I was unsure about going at first but we built a relationship. She helped so much that going there didn't feel like a strain or a pressure.

Now I would say that most people, unless they have known me for a long time, don't know I have dyslexia. It's not something they could pick up every day.

Top Tip from Jordan: I have my own ways of dealing with things and my own ways of working. If you watched me closely, you would probably see that when I write letters or emails at work, I check what I've written probably three or four times – more than other people – but this doesn't stop me from doing them. There's a lot of writing in my job, and when I was at school, I would never have thought I would be able to do this.

Dyslexia helps me because it shows me how to do things a little bit differently. It's changed how I look at things and how I choose to do things, even how I organize myself.

Before I started this job, I worked for a week as a teaching assistant in a school. I felt I was reliving my own school experience. So many things hadn't changed. The kids I was helping had the same issues that I had at school.

A big change needs to happen to support the next generation.

> **Top Tip from Jordan:** I use a lot of colours. Everyone in the office looks at me because I have highlighters everywhere, different coloured pens and different coloured paper, but I find these things help me. That's something my tutor used to do, so I adopted this over time. Whatever helps you is what you should do. You shouldn't think that just because you have dyslexia you can't do something, or you must do something a certain way. You can do it your way.

When I look back to school, I try to think of the positives and I'm grateful for all the support because it allowed me not to be held back by so many barriers. As soon as I left, I was excited because I was given more choices. You can choose at college; you can choose at university. You can challenge yourself and work towards the next stage in your life. You miss having your school friends around you, having been in the same environment for so many years, but besides that you look forward.

The social skills I gained from school have helped me but I've never used algebra or any of those things. No one since I left has asked me to write about Shakespeare.

The one thing I use all the time is something I learnt in English. They told me to make a point, provide evidence of that point, and then explain your point. I use that a lot at work. I don't remember anything else they said, I just

remember that little structure. It helps a lot, especially if you're dealing with something complex.

I see every day as a time to learn. There are certain things that you learn as you walk in the street, especially as a designer. I clock everything as I move around spaces. That is the learning that comes from inside you. There's also a level of learning that you take from a book or from the internet, from somebody more experienced.

Take Every Opportunity

It's important to take every opportunity that life gives. Don't limit yourself because of what you studied. You could do something else. You can always stop and move on to the next thing. Try everything.

I could have decided not to go for this job, and I would have missed out on all the learning I've gained from it. I could have stayed looking for something that was specific and kept me on a narrow path, but I've broadened my horizons. I can always go back if I want to. All work builds connections, and you never know when you're going to need to call on them.

When you're out in the world of work, my advice is to network and stay open-minded. Grab every opportunity. Work is only what you make it. Just because you go to a job every day, that doesn't need to be your work. Your work can be writing, drawing, in your spare time, whatever and whenever you like.

My family has always tried to do everything to help me from when I was diagnosed. That's been a big thing. That and wanting to push myself. We all need that dynamism. As a person of colour there is always something to prove, but I try not to focus on that. I think over the past few years there has been more recognition that people with different backgrounds have been left behind a bit and there's more of an effort to bring them in. I'm not saying enough has been done, but I try to focus on myself personally. If I don't achieve something I move on to the next thing.

With my friends, dyslexia sometimes gives us things to laugh about, especially if I've said or spelt something and everyone is staring at it thinking 'Where did this come from?' I know sometimes when you're young you think dyslexia might stop someone being friends with you, but it hasn't been the case. You don't have to tell someone about dyslexia if you don't want to.

I don't really use social media, and even on WhatsApp I don't think about spelling. My attitude is that no one is giving me a spelling test anymore. People might well make the occasional mistake especially in a longer document. It happens. All you can do is check what you've written, use Spellcheck, and sometimes ask someone else to check it too.

My message to anyone with dyslexia is that if you're getting help it's not going to hold you back, though no one should force support on you. Sometimes the idea of dyslexia can make you feel disempowered, but the choice of how much you want to address it can feel powerful.

I think we can all achieve more than we think we can. When I was at school, I never dreamt I would be able to write a 10,000 word dissertation. There were other options on my course – you could do a presentation, build something, or write a business brief instead. To begin with I thought 'How can I get out of writing this?' but I'm pleased I went ahead. What helped was that we were given a blank canvas about what we wrote about, and I was interested in social housing, so that's what I chose. You have to find a sense of passion. When I found this, I happily did the research, and this got me through. If it had been something I'd been forced to write, I don't think I would have been able to do it.

My Future

I don't know what my future holds. I don't like to limit my goals. As long as I'm happy and healthy and achieving something, and I can look in the mirror and say I feel successful, then that's good enough for me.

I definitely prefer life after school. You have so much more freedom. When you're there, school is everything, but it becomes insignificant once you leave.

Once you're out of it, you don't think about that two out of ten on your spelling test.

If you are struggling with dyslexia, voice your feelings, don't hold them in. Don't sit in silence. Ask for help and then believe in yourself when you have that help. Know that, with the support, you're going to get through.

Even if you don't get the best grades, you're still going to be successful in your own way. Every day you'll learn something new.

> **"After I left school I was excited because I was given more choices. You can choose at college; you can choose at university. You can challenge yourself and work towards the next stage in your life. You miss having your school friends around you, having been in the same environment for so many years, but besides that you look forward."**

CHAPTER 2

Follow Your Heart

EVELYNE CAFFREY
'BUTTERFLY AND HEART'

KATELYNN, 21, MICHIGAN, USA

> **"Presenting at school about dyslexia made me feel proud of who I am and helped me realize I wanted to be a teacher when I was older. I wanted to help other children get the attention they needed."**

When I was a child, learning was hard and there was some bullying. What made me feel good was doing presentations at school about dyslexia to show why I was struggling. I found that when I moved on to high school, the teachers there were interested in what I had to say as well.

Presenting about dyslexia made me feel proud of who I am and helped me realize I wanted to be a teacher when I was older. I wanted to help other children get the attention they needed in class.

Finding a Way

When I left high school, I was kind of scared because my SAT score meant I was denied a place at college. I knew I wanted to be a teacher, but I didn't know how to get there.

My parents and I decided that we were going to investigate different ways for me to reach my goal. We found that Mid-Michigan Community College has an achievement programme for students who don't meet the standards straight out of high school, but who have the potential.

I went there for two semesters, taking classes in general education. Then I transferred over and was given a place at Central Michigan University at Mount Pleasant – so I found that path for getting into university.

I'll be graduating next spring with my education major, pre-kindergarten – or PK – through to sixth grade.

I have had to put in the work, but I have found that university is a lot different from high school. Here I am given maybe a week to turn in a homework assignment. At high school I had to have it done the next day. It is super nice just to have those extra days. I have time to do them and to learn more.

As well as my assignments, this semester I'm taking seven classes. A hefty load.

> **Top Tip from Katelynn:** I have found that if I take an hour or two each night and do a homework assignment or two, my load is just so much easier. Then I give myself the weekend off, just to keep my sanity.

When I'm teaching, I use a whiteboard to help the kids I'm working with learn how to spell a word. They write the word down, using the whiteboard marker, then copy what I have done on their paper. By doing that, the child's spelling has improved. Their reading has also gone up. I worked with a student one-on-one for a good three months last semester, and I was able to bring up her spelling and reading scores.

I'm a very hands-on learner and a visual person. I have been able to show the children I work with what they need to work on, using my techniques. Just seeing the relief in a child's face as they understand what I'm showing them is a reward in itself.

I have given a presentation to my classmates about dyslexia and the Individual Plans students can have to help them. I talked for an hour and a half, and they loved it. I'm so pleased to be able to pass on what I know.

Some things I face difficulties with around school are stress and anxiety. I don't know if they're dyslexia related, but I would say the anxiety probably is. When I'm trying to get organized on the first day of classes, I feel that my head is all over the place. Then I get back to feeling organized and I am much more comfortable. I think it probably takes me a little bit longer to get there than most people.

Another difficulty is that math is still a number one struggle because my numbers will flip, or they disappear, or they all look the same. My reading too – I don't think I've picked up a book since high school. When I read, I feel like I'm riding on a sailboat in the middle of the ocean, trying and not managing to go over the waves.

Schoolwork is so stressful for me, and I put my heart and energy into this. This means that if I make friends throughout the school year then fine, but I don't ever try to get close with them just because I don't always have time to go out and be a social butterfly.

I have a very few close friends that I talk with. I prefer a small group. Less drama. Any social media, I always have my siblings read it to check it sounds OK. They have been my number one supporters, as well as my parents.

I've had to do most of my learning on my own. I learn as I go every day. I think I'm like my parents. We are go-getter people – we get things done but we learn at the same time.

Keep Organized

I have always tried to keep organized. Last semester, I was juggling a full-time schedule, being a swim coach for a high school, working with my dad helping him wire up stores with his electrical company, and working at a school. I was going somewhere every single day. I didn't know what day it was.

Now, if I have to be somewhere at three o'clock and I don't get there right on time, it's fine. I have learnt to let go a little bit.

The strategy I would pass on to anyone at high school reading this is to say just keep going. There shouldn't be anything stopping you from doing what you want in life and getting to where you want to go.

Top Tip from Katelynn: If you feel like you're lacking confidence, ask yourself what you're struggling with. Seek help and find someone to get you on your way. Someone with patience. It just takes a lot of patience.

My life is feeling pretty good right now. I feel I'm ready to be in a classroom and start my career and teach. It's kind of hard holding back and not being able to do that straightaway. From when I was in second grade,* I felt I was meant to be a teacher. I noticed how well I worked with kids, and that I would have more to give them when I was older. I even feel that I have a gift. I want to be able to share that with others.

> **"The strategy I would pass on to anyone at high school reading this is to say just keep going. There shouldn't be anything stopping you from doing what you want in life and getting to where you want to go."**

* Seven or eight years old

WILL, 20, VICTORIA, AUSTRALIA

> **"I want to work with kids, especially kids who are troubled and starting to go down a dangerous path with drug abuse, theft, and crime. I find that kind of work very, very satisfying."**

At school I faced a lot of bullying. This meant I grew up disliking bad things happening to good people. I want to fight injustice and have an impact on this in my work.

School was easier when I started to fit in socially, in late high school. It was also where I worked out that I could achieve more than other people thought I could.

Since I left, life's been good. After some time working at the Woolworths grocery store, I went back to my old school to work in sports training. At the same time, I qualified to do some swim teaching, low-level coaching and mentoring, and fitness training. I'm now working as a lifeguard and about to do a swim teaching qualification.

My goal after this is to join the police to do a youth liaison role. I would be working with kids, especially kids who are troubled and starting to go down a dangerous path with drug abuse, theft, and crime. I find that kind of work very, very satisfying.

The exciting news is I've put my application into Victoria Police and, if everything goes to plan, I should be at the Police Academy within the next month or so. I've passed all the writing tests, the maths tests, and the physical tests. I'm currently waiting on my psychological evaluation to come back, and that should happen within the next couple of days. After this there will be an interview, then 16–20 weeks at the academy doing training and learning the law and another nine months on the job training. Then I will be deployed to the closest city to where I live.

I've come a long way, even from my later time in high school when I had one teacher in particular who basically told me I should drop out because I would never amount to anything. She said I should focus on getting a trade or getting any job anywhere. That was a bit of a downer at the time, but I think she's probably the main reason why I completed my last school year. I made the decision to prove her wrong. I stayed at school and did the higher level of exams, the VCA, which can lead to university. I scored in the high 70s, and that was quite surprising.

Working Hard

I worked hard that whole time. I was working to my own schedule, not what the teachers were expecting me to do. I was working at odd hours, and I was allowed to use a computer for all my exams, with extra time allocated for writing and correcting my work.

All of that helped level the playing field quite a bit and essentially made my work legible for people to read. My handwriting still isn't that great, and that had been a major barrier, but Spellcheck helps me a lot.

Having worked at a school, I find I enjoy interacting with people and problem solving most of all. I like having almost a chaplaincy role, especially after kids have been through fights and big losses. Even in sport when kids are losing, it's important they know how to deal with that properly.

In the past few years, I've been volunteering with a local programme that's run by the police called Blue Light. I'm helping with a programme in one of the bigger towns in the area. There's a lot of youth crime and this is a sports programme to try to encourage young people to take a different path. There are sports activities, gym sessions, and camps to encourage positive behaviour. It's very rewarding and helped me see the pathway that I want to pursue.

I think that teacher at school thought I would end up on the dole, taking a cheque from the government. What she said and everything I went through taught me not to give up on what I wanted to do. I faced a lot of stress and anxiety at the time, but I found a way of seeing what I wanted to achieve in life. Then I pursued it to the best of my ability. I forced myself to do well.

When I left school, there was a big sense of relief, especially when I had completed all my exams. I also felt a little bit of foreboding because I had to work out what I was going to do next, so there was excitement and nerves.

At school I learnt resilience and to follow my own instincts. The subjects I learnt at school didn't help me afterwards, but what has helped is learning how best to

respond to a situation that doesn't suit me or my skills, trying to prove people wrong.

Most of my learning and understanding of the world in general was done at home, through discussions with friends and family, particularly my parents, and from the internet which is a massive learning aid. This especially helped with my police exam and the maths component, as I dropped maths in Year 9. I essentially had to teach myself maths from scratch, based on internet tutorials. I found this much easier than learning at school because I was able to go at my own pace. If I watch something and it doesn't make sense to me, I can go and read about it somewhere else and find 100 different ways to see the same problem.

Coping with Work

Unlike school, I have rarely had problems at work. When I was working at the school, I had to do a lot of writing, like lesson plans and lesson summaries, reports on kids, that kind of thing. I noticed the others worked through these things a lot faster and navigated the systems a lot quicker than I did, but over time I was able to improve and figure out shortcuts. Spellcheck was a lifesaver again, and I only needed to use my handwriting to take notes.

Generally, I like this idea that there are very few things in life you can control, so I focus on what I can control and influence and move through life in that manner. Something else that helps me progress is technology. Having the world's knowledge on my phone is very helpful, especially when I'm trying to figure out words and how to phrase things when I'm writing them down.

A lot of my mates take the piss out of me because of my dyslexia and the way I write and getting my numbers back to front. I was trying to help build a bar in my mate's shed and I was writing half of the measurements down the wrong way around. They eventually said, 'You're too dyslexic for this. Let someone else take over', which was fair enough. I rarely post anything on social media, because it's more writing, and I'm not a fan of the way it makes people act. I watched cyberbullying happening from afar in school. So I have my own thoughts that can stay with me. No one else needs to know them.

Top Tip from Will: My family has supported me with my dyslexia. Families have to be understanding and encouraging. Even if advice seems to fall on deaf ears, that stuff can stick in the back of people's heads when it's put out there.

When I look around me, the people with the most success are the ones who give 100 per cent effort to the small things – showing up early or on time, that kind of thing. Especially at work, people do appreciate it.

Life after school can be daunting if you're not prepared for it. Luckily, I had a clear goal, which was to go into the police. Everything I've done was done to assist me in that goal. In my work as a lifeguard, I can find myself interacting with volatile people. It turns out a lot of folk don't like being told not to dive into the shallow end.

If you're struggling at school now, life does get better. If you can find like-minded people who share your values and understand you, this helps no matter what else you're dealing with. It may sometimes seem to you that life won't improve but, from my experience, it certainly does.

> **"The people with the most success are the ones who give 100 per cent effort in regard to the small things – showing up early or on time. Especially at work, people do appreciate it."**

SAMUEL, 19, PRINCE EDWARD ISLAND, CANADA

“I had always wanted to drive from when I was young, either being on a tractor on a farm or running a bulldozer or excavator on a building site. Even when I was a kid I just hopped in when I had the chance and tried to do my best behind the wheel.”

When I graduated and left school I felt like there was a weight lifted off my back. At the same time, I knew that life was going to become a lot harder because I would have to be working and paying for my food and everything. It almost seemed like it was more stressful than going to school every day, when you don’t have to worry about money all the time. That made me wish I was still in kindergarten, but not in all the English or science classes that followed.

At 18 I started looking at colleges I could go to, but there were no courses that really excited me.

I knew if I wasn’t excited about something, it wouldn’t work out. It would just mean more struggle.

Instead, I took a three-month course to drive construction equipment. The learning was more hands-on compared to the classroom. This was by far the best subject I’ve ever studied and the best results I’ve ever had on a report card.

All my merits were in the 90s. That felt different. I didn't even recognize that feeling.

I called my mom and told her about my grades. My parents were really excited for me because I don't think they ever thought they were going to hear those words come out of my mouth.

Right after that I started working for a construction company and straightaway I knew I had chosen the right work. I found running this equipment was exciting and fun. I had always wanted to drive from when I was young, either driving a tractor on a farm or running a bulldozer or excavator on a building site. Even when I was a kid I just hopped in when I had the chance and tried to do my best behind the wheel.

Seeing Things Differently

I'm good at what I do. Sometimes I think the way I see things is different from other people I'm working with. Once we were laying down bricks for a driveway, and they tried to shape the drive in a way to make it look good, but that meant we would have had to cut the bricks into a lot of pieces to fit. This would have turned into a difficult job that would have taken a lot of time. I saw straightaway that if we laid them down in a different way it would still look good, and we wouldn't have to cut the bricks.

At times I think of new ways to operate the equipment using the attachments that are provided. This saves time and the results are better.

Fun at Work

One of the things I like best about my work is the people I work with. There's lots of fun. It's not always serious 24/7. You can have good conversations with people, and you can just work and talk and work some more.

I have a lot of confidence around people. I don't know if it's from being involved in so many sports and extra activities after school when I was younger, but I know how to talk to others and I'm not nervous to go up to them. I could talk to someone walking down the street and say 'Hey, how you doing?' when I've never met them in my life. I would say the social aspect of school, getting to know people and how to deal with them, definitely helped me.

The only times I don't know how to talk to people at work is when I almost feel like I've been cornered – like when they say something to you, but you don't know what they mean, and you don't know how to respond. In those moments I haven't been able to find the vocabulary to say what I want back to them.

Since I've left school, I haven't read a lot or written a lot of words, and I've forgotten how to write some things I used to know. The biggest way this affects me is when I'm trying to text someone. Then I hope I've guessed a spelling close enough so that Autocorrect works. If what I've written is so far off the spelling, what I send makes no sense because I didn't know how to spell it, and they don't know what I mean. Luckily people I know well guess what I'm trying to say and I think my texting is improving.

Sometimes I can't text people, just because I don't know how to spell what I wanted to say. I know that a lot of people like to text and not call, but I prefer to call someone instead. They feel like you're weird for calling them, but I won't know how to say what I want to in a text, and I don't want to feel left out.

With my girlfriend sometimes I write things, and it doesn't even make sense to her. What I have written is not even close to what I wanted to say. The good thing is that she usually works out what I'm saying. I don't ever try to post on social media, but that isn't a loss as I have enough people in my life. I don't need to go reaching for more.

Looking back to school, I realize how much fun it actually was. I never realized it in the moment, how many friends were around me. I changed schools halfway through and went to a nonprofit tutoring centre. I did quite well, compared to what my grades were before. It was almost like starting from kindergarten again.

I think I probably could have tried a little bit harder with my education. I could have done more homework, even though I hated it. It probably would have helped me a bit more with my future if I'd tried to succeed more.

In the school I was at before I moved, I felt that perhaps the teachers hadn't been properly told what dyslexic students needed to help them learn. Sometimes kids couldn't speak up about this because they didn't feel comfortable enough talking to their teachers in that way. Schools need to be more open to what the students need.

Some students in the first high school gave me a hard time. I found that in the second school this was a lot better. They didn't see me for how I was learning. They saw me for the person I was.

Now that I'm an adult I think certain school courses, especially math and maybe a little bit of English, help me now. I know that math helped because I need to use it for work. Even the cooking we learnt at school helped me live on my own.

Try Your Hardest

Top Tip from Samuel: If you're still at school, you should try your hardest. When you don't know something, ask. Don't hide that you don't understand. You'll be left not knowing and then they try to make you learn something else on top. You don't want to go three or four things down the line and you're still trying to make sense of the first one.

When I was younger, I found it harder to ask. As I got older it was easier. I became more confident. It was important to admit to myself that I had dyslexia, and I couldn't change that.

My parents knew that for me to succeed, I had to have the support in place. Without it I would have had a hard time at school. I had an iPad in school for help with writing and reading, I had a computer. I had some extra support staff, and if you didn't understand something, you could go to them, and they might be able to help you figure it out. Or they might be able to work with the teachers to create a learning plan.

If someone you're supporting has dyslexia, ask them what they need to help them learn more, not what you think they need. See if that works.

If your children love sports or something else, make compromises with them to do some work, but at the same time, enjoy life. So they get to go outside and play for a half an hour as a reward, then come in and read five or ten pages of a book. That type of thing.

> **Top Tip from Samuel:** I find as you get older you don't change from when you were young. You've got to have that mix of doing stuff that you enjoy, and things that might help you learn but you might not enjoy as much, because if you're more excited and motivated, you'll normally learn better.

I'd suggest anyone reading this finds something that they're good at for work, something they enjoy. Then it shouldn't matter about the money you get, except that you need to support yourself. If your brain can do it, you should pursue it 100 per cent. Don't worry about going to university for four to six years. Do what you love.

> “Don’t hide that you don’t understand. You’ll be left not knowing and then they try to make you learn something else on top. You don’t want to go three or four things down the line and you’re still trying to make sense of the first one. When I was younger, I found it harder to ask. As I got older it was easier. I became more confident.”

ANWEN, 17, CARMARTHEN, WALES

“Struggling at school made me want to find something else to focus on that I felt good about. Being outdoors on my bike feels like a relief and an escape. It’s my thing to do well in.”

School doesn’t show you all the options in life. They push you to do A Levels* and a degree, and they don’t tell you about jobs that are hands-on and a bit different.

I knew when I was at school that even if you don’t have a degree, you’re not dumb. You still have a brain; you just can’t spell. Everyone has things they’re good at and bad at. You can be bad at running, and no one sees that, but because you have dyslexia it’s seen as more of a big deal.

Mum kept on telling me, ‘It’s not the end of the world. There are so many other options in life’. Now I’ve left school I know she wasn’t lying.

For so many reasons, I loved school. Loads of the teachers were lovely and the social side was great. School gave me the chance to prove myself in lots of ways.

My mum is top notch. She always says that everyone has the same size brain, we just use them differently. I think I’m someone who wasn’t good in the classroom but I’m hands-on and love outdoor activities. All of this comes

* A Levels are exams taken in most of the UK at the age of 18

from struggling at school, which takes up so much of your life. This made me want to find something else to focus on that I felt good about. Being outdoors feels like a relief and an escape. It's my thing to do well in.

I've always been super sporty. I'm now focusing on cycling and I'm hopefully going to end up with a cycling career. I am training with a coach, and waitressing on the side to make some extra money.

Sporting Life

I think a career in sport is one of the hardest things in the world to aim for. Who wouldn't choose to be paid to play the sport they love? Only 2 per cent make it if you're trying to be a professional footballer. As soon as you're not what they want, you're gone. Once you have an injury you can be done, and that's scary, but it doesn't put me off. I train twice a day, doing 16 or 17 hours on a bike every week and running and swimming in between that. I make sure I do physio.

If you want it, you've got to work for it.

I do off road cycling, especially cyclocross and mountain biking. I'm in the Welsh squad and I'm hoping to get into the GB squad next year.

I just love cycling. I work super hard, but it's worth it. I have lovely parents who support me so much and I couldn't do it without them.

My parents have three girls and a boy. We were all put into the sport that you typically would expect us to like, so the girls were put into netball, swimming, and ice skating and my brother went into football, rugby, and cycling. I'm not a tomboy but I wanted to cycle like my brother. I wanted to be like him.

I like just being outdoors. It's so refreshing and it's healthy. To be able to just go out on your bike and risk a little bit, go downhill in what I call 'big fat drops'.

When I was at school in lessons, people sometimes said to me, 'Why are you still on that question?', but actual friends didn't ask that. Looking back, I didn't take the learning very seriously. I didn't want to feel stupid, so I made a joke of it all at some points, and I probably did mess around a bit too much.

Studying What I Loved

I loved science and decided to do triple science. People were saying, 'Is this a good idea? You might struggle', but I did it and came out with an ABC, so this was proof that even with dyslexia if you work you can get to where you want to be. It's harder but you can get there.

I made friends with two girls who were in all my science classes. They were unbelievable and they had full A stars in their GCSEs.* It was a bit disappointing opening my results next to them. My mum said that I needed to

* GCSEs are taken in most of the UK at the age of 16

understand I'd worked hard and passed all my predicted grades and how much of an achievement that was for me.

Help at School

The biggest help to me was that when I was very young, I went to a dyslexia school, Tomorrow's Generation, instead of going to an ordinary primary. For me it was a place where everyone was the same. It was fun and they don't make you feel stupid. You could spell cat wrong, and they just would be like, 'That's fine', and help you. By the time I went to secondary school I was at the reading level I should be at.

When I was there, my mum was sometimes getting calls saying I wasn't turning up for lessons and she said, 'Well, pull her out of them because I don't think she needs to be in there'. Then I would go and sit with my PE teachers. They helped me so much. They were great and they still are. Every time I'm on TV when I'm racing, they text me saying, 'We'll be watching'.

Having a talent, like sport or music, is great, but there's just not enough of it in school. It feels like there might be one lesson in the whole week, and my school was an amazing high school.

For years I would beg my mum to homeschool me. She always said no. She knew how sociable I was, and she said I would hate it after a while. Still, she spent a lot of time with me at weekends. We did bits and bobs, arts and crafts, things like crochet, just to make me feel normal.

Then she might sit down with me to do a little bit of spelling, but this was somewhere I felt happy to do this. I knew she wasn't judging me or making me feel thick or writing down my marks. She was just wanting the best for me. At school if you do something wrong, they're not helping you, they're grading you.

> **Top Tip from Anwen:** At home we used to play Scrabble, and we had a rule that as long as it sounded right and we knew it sounded like a word then that was OK. So it was correct in a sense but not actually correct. It was all part of the message from our parents that we weren't stupid, just good at other stuff.

Dyslexia can make me worry in other areas of my life. I waitress in a Korean Chinese restaurant and when I turned up for the first time I was scared. I looked at the words we had to use for the food and the spelling of them and they gave me a pen to take down people's orders, and I thought, 'Oh, my goodness'. Then I found out you take the orders to the till and the person on the till puts the orders in with the correct spellings, so that was OK.

Sometimes one of the customers points to something on the menu and asks me, 'What's this?', and in the past I wouldn't have a clue. So my mum sat with me and went over the menu and we'd practise it. After a few shifts, I was like, 'OK, I get this'.

Dyslexia doesn't affect my friendships. My best friend I've known since nursery, and the others are in sports, so they don't care if you're in the thick set or smart set – they just want you to play football. My best friend will read my texts and know exactly what I mean even with my spelling. Dyslexia doesn't affect my relationship with my boyfriend or my posts on social media, though I am always sitting with my mum saying, 'How do you spell this?'

I believe that education needs to change. Schools need to realize that they need to stop pushing so much. Reading and writing are so huge there. Except for maths, it feels like that's all there is and they make it seem like that's how it will be for the rest of your life.

Top Tip from Anwen: Something else that's important is knowing that if you have dyslexia you need to take double the time with your work. I'd sit there and spell a word and spell the word again and spell it again. Things don't go into my mind when I read them. I have to read them three or four times. You have to put in the hours.

When it came to deciding about sixth form I was like, nah, I need some time away from lessons. Life now feels like a relief. I don't feel I'm being judged on the things I'm doing.

My Second Career

If you don't see me in the Olympics, I'll be delivering babies. My middle sister had a baby who came early. She was just three pounds, so little and tiny. When we turned up, this midwife was holding this little, tiny baby. It made me think that working with newborns would be so lovely. Then it hit me: 'I've just decided on my other career'.

Working as a midwife would mean being with people, talking and helping, being hands-on, and science was one of my better subjects at school. So if it all goes wrong with sport, that's my other option. I've been accepted to go on that course next year. When I think about myself, I know I'm not a classroom person and that's why I chose midwifery. If I can't cycle, that's what I'll do.

My advice to anyone is to be confident in yourself and know what you're good at. Mum always says to me, 'Think about what you like. Think about what you can do'. We all find some things hard and some things good. It's the

KERI BAKER

same for everyone, they're just different things. Struggling in the classroom is not the end of the world. If it's not your strong suit, just try your best and remind yourself of your positives, because you have loads. Everyone does.

"My advice to anyone is to be confident in yourself and know what you're good at. Mum always says to me, 'Think about what you like. Think about what you can do.'"

MOLLY, 23, STIRLINGSHIRE, SCOTLAND/ YORK, ENGLAND

> "Everyone was like, 'Go to university', but I thought college would be more practical and I heard they were good with helping people with dyslexia, an important point for me."

Life is so much better after school. You feel like you're getting your life going, which is a boost. You get to focus on what you're interested in.

At school there are lots of hormones and lots of anxieties in one big swelling pool. When you're out of that, you're able to consider yourself and look inwardly a bit more. You meet new people, hear new viewpoints, have new experiences. There's less ignorance, and the ignorance there is, you learn to deal with.

There were some good things about school. One of the best things was that they let me do some work experience at a local college to see how the department worked. I also helped in music technology classes in school as a sort of class assistant.

I did night courses at a college off my own back to find out more about sound design. This was helpful too.

After school I applied to university and college. Everyone was like, 'Go to university', where I had been accepted to do Archaeology and Criminology, but I decided to do a

Higher National Diploma (HND)* in Sound Production in Forth Valley College in Stirling. I thought college would be more practical and I heard they were good with helping people with dyslexia, an important point for me.

I ended up living at home while I studied, which was great because I didn't have to get a job to pay for my rent. I did this course for two years and it was epic. The best choice I ever made.

Choosing a Practical Course

College was so hands-on. There were some written projects, but the course was mainly practical. Theory was taught at the same time, so it made sense. This was a great stepping stone for me. I ended up volunteering with Audio Engineering Scotland and the BBC – the college was good at getting us these opportunities.

I left with an A in my HND and applied to the Glasgow School of Art where I studied for two years for a BA (Hons) in Sound for the Moving Image.

Excellent Support

I loved the School of Art. My supervisor was brilliant with me. She was also my dyslexic liaison, and we had a good chat about once a fortnight about how things were going

* HND is a vocational qualification

and if anything could be improved. They were really on the ball.

At one stage I started to struggle. There was a lot more writing at university and a lot more reading. I found I was staying up until three in the morning trying to do pre-readings for lectures the next day.

After a couple of weeks, I went to my tutor and said, 'I'm just really tired. I'm staying up till 3 am and then I have my lectures'. She told me I didn't have to do that. I shouldn't burn myself out. That was great advice, and it put me in the right mindset. I realized getting sleep and being able to focus in lectures was way more important. I didn't retain stuff from reading anyway. I would have to read it over and over again which wouldn't work for me, as my reading speed is low.

I decided to put my mental health and ability to focus above everything else. So I went to the lectures, and if I needed any extra information, I read up on a couple of relevant points afterwards. This meant I could learn much more easily.

It was great that my lecturers understood dyslexia. Everything was printed on green backgrounds or was in green writing, the colour I read best from. They gave me an extension if I needed it. They were there to help.

The Glasgow School of Art helped me a lot with my dissertation which was on forensic audio techniques. This means exploring audio recordings to see if they can help with criminal cases, and clearing up audio to see if it has been edited or tampered with.

There was a lot of reading in my dissertation, and I was quite scared about it, but I had a choice of writing half the words and doing a project alongside it. I chose that option and I graduated with a 2:1.*

> **Top Tip from Molly:** Altogether I've had such a good experience with higher education, and I know other people haven't. Finding out which educational places give good support is vital.

After this I needed a break as I was getting burnt out, so I took a year out. Then I did a master's at York University on Forensic Speech Science, the same subject as my dissertation. I had become super interested in this. I had shifted from wanting to be a sound designer to wanting to work in forensics.

Forensic speech science can play an important role in the criminal justice system. Sometimes, if audio is heavily distorted, transcripts are needed for juries: they can have an audio playing and the transcript alongside it for comparison. Sometimes we help the police. If you have a known suspect on a police recording, we can analyse the speech and say whether it is likely to be the same person or not. Sometimes we are needed to explain to a jury what we've done and why we've come to the conclusions we have.

* The second highest degree classification in the UK

Failing Maths

There are times when I think I should have left school earlier and gone to college earlier because I found the work more practical. Other times I think staying at school gave me a more rounded knowledge base. Some parts of school I look back on fondly, others I don't. I failed my maths three times. Once I walked out an hour and a half early from a two-hour exam. I didn't find English easy, but reading something that interested me was helpful. My dad sometimes pre-read my work for me and helped me with spelling and grammar and that was so useful.

At school I always found it hard to memorize poems, but I found a way, involving making connections in my brain. This helped me remember what I think of as mumbo jumbo at university too. I would create images to flash up in my mind what I was trying to remember. It's finding a way that suits you if you're dyslexic, working out your strategies.

Top Tip from Molly: One of my strategies was asking my reader/scribe at school to read out my maths and English questions three times. I had my highlighter pens ready and on the second reading I followed the words along with my finger, making sure I highlighted the key words. I still use my highlighters now. I still ask myself, 'What's the key message in this question?'

My school always told me not to listen to music while I'm studying, but I found some music works well. I had playlists for different aspects of my work. Without it I could find myself staring at a blank wall. I listened to the weirdest things – French hip hop and Dutch rap were two of them, so I had that lyrical bass in the background, quite fast paced, but I couldn't understand the words, so I wasn't able to sing along and get distracted.

When I left school, I was ready to move on. I think for a lot of us with dyslexia, by the time you get to your last year you feel like you're in a rut and you just want a change. High school is rough enough for the best of us, though I did like the structure I learnt there and that helped me create structure for my master's and any freelance work.

Help Your Mental Health

I have tried doing some part-time work while studying. I was waitressing at one stage at the weekends, but it was terrible. I found I needed a break. You get kind of burnt out. Again, I learnt that you need to prioritize.

> **Top Tip from Molly:** Make decisions that are good for your mental health, and if you're feeling drained make yourself a cup of tea. You're not going to miss learning something in those ten minutes while you're taking a brain break.

One thing I learnt from my master's is not to be afraid of things I'd failed in the past. There's maths in my master's which I hated at school, and I thought I would never do again, but in my master's I mostly understand it. That's because it is presented in a real-world perspective. I can understand the implications of the questions they're asking, and it's not just X plus Y equals Z.

I don't submit any written work if it hasn't been looked over. I have a sticker on my work now for spelling and grammar. That means if they can make out what I've written, they're not allowed to mark me down for it.

One good thing about being dyslexic is the way it affects my friendships. There are some other neurodivergent people in my master's class. We compare our differences, and rather than disappearing down academic rabbit holes, we tend to talk about broader things. I'll talk about feelings or have a different viewpoint in a conversation.

My brain is wired differently. Some people call it a learning disability, but it's just a learning difference. It just means I need a bit of extra help. My lecturers send out the PowerPoints 24 hours early because I can't flip through them like other people can.

Top Tip from Molly: You need to stand up for yourself. I mentioned in all of my interviews: 'I have dyslexia. What can you do to support me?' The most helpful thing was that one of my lecturers videoed the lectures for me.

I don't post on social media. I think it's partly because my spelling is awful. I laugh about it, but it's genuinely terrible. The other reason is that I'm living my life, and I don't feel the need to post about it.

If you're trying to support a loved one with dyslexia, my advice would be to be patient with them. Know that they're probably either going to be silent about it or talk your ear off about it. Sometimes life will be overwhelming. Sometimes they'll need your help solving a problem and sometimes they know what to do. Sometimes they'll snap at you if you're trying to support them.

Deep inside, even though I can laugh about my bad spelling, I feel sensitive about it. I can laugh about it more now than I could when I was 16. If someone is trying to help it won't be an attack, but it might feel like one.

I think dyslexia has made me more caring towards others, more aware of their difficulties. I am more vigilant for other people who may be struggling.

Hopefully my future holds good things for me. Hopefully I'll be helping people. That's why I shifted from sound design to doing something more active in the judicial system. It does feel amazing studying something I enjoy.

I love what I do, and I wouldn't change my dyslexia for anything, even though it can be a hindrance sometimes. I can think differently. I can think of things that are relevant to the conversation that other people won't think about, things that are related to an academic paper that's just been talked about. I'll be like, 'But what if they did it this way?' I'm always having crazy ideas – some won't come to anything, but some of them might just work.

"I think dyslexia has made me more caring towards others, more aware of their difficulties. I I am more vigilant for other people who may be struggling."

OLIVER, 23, CANTERBURY, ENGLAND

"I liked knowing I had a responsible job on the railways. I had to deal with anything that went wrong, including track circuit failures. This meant that suddenly I had to put my knowledge into practice. Every day was different."

My secondary school pushed everyone into going to university who had the chance. I think they do that to make themselves look good. Even if you're clear you don't want to go, they tell you, 'Apply anyway, just to keep your options open'. I think that pressures people into seeing university as their only choice if they're not sure what to do, instead of thinking, 'There are loads of things I can do for my career'.

I chose not to go, and I'm probably in the same position that I would have been if I'd gone. Plus, I'd have a lot less money now because of the cost of university fees.

Looking back, I can see why teachers weren't too keen on my choices, but everything worked out fine. For my first 18 years, our house backed onto a railway, and I always loved railways. My nursery school backed out onto the railway line as well. I spent hours looking out onto it, as well as playing with my massive wooden train set.

My uncle and my granddad are both railway enthusiasts and they were a big influence.

Top Tip from Oliver: When I was 15, I did work experience on the London Underground, seeing where they controlled the signals, looking round the depot, and being given a cab ride at the front of a train. I watched closely what everyone was doing. Work experience is a great idea, especially if it gives you a good overview of everything involved in a job.

Instead of A Levels, I went to college to study a BTEC* Level 3 in Computer Science. After that I kept applying for jobs; I was unemployed for about three months. I was quite relaxed about that because I knew what I wanted to do, but my mum was getting concerned.

Some of the time I was unemployed I was in Wales volunteering on a heritage railway. That was so enjoyable because of the camaraderie and I learnt things that I could apply to a job on a mainline railway.

Finally, I succeeded with a job application, and I was given a job as a crossing keeper. This meant working in a former signal box, ensuring the safe running of trains over a level crossing. You're there to close the gates to road traffic, enabling the trains to go past, and to make sure the whole area is safe.

It was a lovely job, in a lovely part of the world. I had support if I needed it, but most of the time I was there on my own. I liked my own company and knowing I had a responsible job. I had to deal with anything that went wrong, like track circuit failures. This meant that suddenly

* Work-related qualification

I had to put my knowledge into practice. Every day was different.

Eventually that job was automated. Now I'm a signaller. For this I had to go to signalling school for a 12-week residential course. Along with the theory in the classroom we had morning and evening simulator practice to make sure we could do the job. We had to learn the entire railway rulebook and get tested on it inside out.

Because I have dyslexia I was given reasonable adjustments for this. There were seven or eight of us in the class and if any of us struggled with any part of it we could speak to the trainers who were really good. If I couldn't get the notes down, I talked to them afterwards to go through everything.

I think it helped that I had previously been working on the railway as this meant I knew the basics. It would have been harder if I'd walked in straight from the street.

With this job, I have more responsibilities. I make decisions that are vital to maintain the safe running of the railway. I act on rail defects and signal failures and all sorts that happen that people don't know about. If a farmer rings up and wants to cross a railway line with their sheep or their cattle, we tell them if it is safe to cross the railway line or not. The smooth running of the trains and safety are always our priorities.

Learning on the Job

I find that doing the job teaches me a lot. It's like learning to drive. Even when you pass your test, you don't really know how to do it until you get some experience.

When I look back, college especially was good because we were given a lot of freedom, with free periods and a bit of breathing space. We called our college teachers by their first names and that helped us feel we were being treated like adults.

A lot of people at my college went on to apprenticeships and I'm a big believer in apprenticeships that are high quality. It's a great way to get educated while you're getting experience in industry and being paid as well.

I don't see myself as a highflyer by any means, but I have a job that's important for the country, with good working conditions. I am happy with my quality of life, and to be honest I think that's probably what a lot of people want. Then you can springboard into enjoying other things you want to do in your spare time. If I had pushed myself more academically I don't think I would have enjoyed my life more. Also, I'm not someone who likes being told what to do: 'You've got to write an essay on this', that kind of thing.

I much prefer life after school, but I didn't hate school. I was quite fortunate in that my parents pushed for me to get a lot of support. This meant I had an hour a week of one-on-one help from when I was 10 until I left at 16. A teacher called Lois came in and she really helped me when everyone else was in their citizenship class.

School gave me a laptop to use if I wanted to. There

was also a teaching assistant who worked across a few students in the classrooms.

My dyslexia was quite severe. At 11 I had a reading age of an eight-year-old. I still remember spelling the word 'fire' wrong. I put 'fyer' or something like that. I also remember never being given a pen licence because my handwriting wasn't neat enough, but it was never going to be good.

At school dyslexia can make you feel ostracized if you have extra support, with people asking why you have certain things, such as extra time in exams. It's important to own that you have dyslexia, not to be meek about it; focus on doing well rather than worrying about what they think.

I also suggest you make the most of school that you can. It's not the end of the world if you don't get the best grades, but don't flunk your exams on purpose. Do what you can because it is important.

When I left school I felt quite excited for the future. These days I think my spelling is pretty good, but I have to look at words visually, not sound them out. If I look at a word I can usually tell if it's not spelt right. I don't read books, but if you gave me an article I could go through it and give you a summary of it. I enjoy writing but usually I would use a computer as I was taught to touch type at my local dyslexia centre. I became interested in audiobooks after leaving formal education. My local library has a good selection on a mobile app. I'm just listening to Harry Potter which I wouldn't have read. They are really good.

Top Tip from Oliver: I use a Dictaphone rather than writing something down I don't have to. I think you can express yourself better that way. Voice notes are far better for me than texting. You can say more, and people can hear your tone of voice. I don't say anything much on social media and I don't use it too much. I have compared my feeds and my friends' feeds and mine is far more video and image based, less words.

Some things we learn at school are underrated, like dealing with authority, but there's a lot they teach that feels completely pointless. It's fine enjoying poetry, but why would we need to memorize it? It doesn't prove anything except that you can remember.

There's a lot I learnt there that I'll never need again, like maths without a calculator, and then there's stuff we should have been taught, like the Cycling Proficiency.

Since I've been at work, I don't think dyslexia has been a hindrance. It just means a different way of doing things. We often have to fill in a form for overnight engineering works. Most people print out a blank form and fill it in by hand, but it's much easier for me to use the computer. Being good with a computer is very important if you're dyslexic, as this can help with spelling and writing issues.

The way I learn most is being around other people and seeing how they operate. Their experience teaches me a lot. I'm fairly young in the job that I do, especially in my area, and there are some people who have been there for 50 years. It's good just to ask them questions and hear what they say about how the workplace has changed. That gives you far better insights than if you just sat there and said nothing. If there's an issue you're tackling and you can't find the answer written down in the rule book, you can ask the person on either side of you what their thoughts are. You build a bank of knowledge for yourself.

Work Is Enjoyable

One thing no one tells you in school is that work is enjoyable. You get in your head that it's going to be a very serious thing in a shirt and tie and you do your job and go home. Things are serious, but you can still enjoy the work and have a good conversation with a co-worker.

Arriving Late

One issue I still have with dyslexia is that when I'm meeting friends, I show up late. Some of them purposely tell me we're meeting an hour earlier so they're not waiting around. I was terrible at time management at school, and I haven't improved much since.

If I was helping someone with dyslexia, I would look into the support measures that could be put in place and make sure the school is aware of them. They won't want to spend the money on this but push for it. That was life-changing for me. Help from someone working only with you, who understands dyslexia, going at your pace, makes all the difference. If they are finding things tough advise them to focus on English and maths for their GCSEs and then add anything else they enjoy.

When it comes to after school, I wouldn't put pressure on anyone to go to university. Let them come to their own decision. My parents were very good with that. There are so many other routes someone can go down to become a well-rounded individual.

When you have started work it's worth telling your employer you are dyslexic. Good employers should find a way to make reasonable adjustments. You can be a good, productive employee with dyslexia.

There's a lot of pressure on you at 16 to make decisions, and for me, deciding to go to college rather than stay in school and do A Levels is one of the best decisions I have made. Life after school is much better. It's partly the freedom, especially with shift work, and it's partly getting paid. Still now I can be on a day off and thinking, 'It's Wednesday and I'm not at work and I have money to spend on stuff I want.' Unbelievable.

"The way I learn most is being around other people and seeing how they operate. I'm fairly young in the job that I do, especially in my area, and there are some people who have been there for 50 years. It's good just to ask them questions and hear what they say about how the workplace has changed. That gives you far better insights than if you just sat there and said nothing. You build a bank of knowledge for yourself."

SARAH, 18, QUEBEC, CANADA

> **"At my college one professor told us he has dyslexia, autism, and ADHD. He wants people to know that there are professors like this. That was really cool for me and made a big impact on how I viewed myself as a student. Him sharing his story made me realize I could do more things in my life. Perhaps I could become a Professor of Music as well."**

In my lifetime, I've heard a lot of music because my sister listens to it constantly. My sister has severe disabilities and uses a wheelchair. We have ways of communicating with her and we know she can hear music. As a result, she listens to music around the clock, as it's one of the things she loves. This is one reason I'm constantly singing throughout the house and humming to myself. It means music has always been a big part of my life. I can hear patterns within tunes, and I can often recognize the notes that will be coming next.

When I left high school, I decided to be open-minded about where the future would take me. I studied Music Performance for my gap year, and fell in love with it. I received a scholarship to continue, and I'm now doing a four-year programme. My music programme has made me happier and has given me a better understanding of how I'm capable. I have always heard things in music that I wanted to explain, but didn't know how to put into words. It was like looking at a colour and seeing all the depths and shades within it, instead of seeing 'blue'. One example is I now know that if a piece of music in a minor key ends with a major third, it's called a Picardy. Suddenly you find out that what your ears have heard has a name, and you're like, 'Oh, yeah'.

One-on-One Time

I'm in one of the top colleges in Canada, with a limited number of students so there's more one-on-one time. The teachers believe in us, so they push us hard, but there's a real community there. In my last year of high school, I'd been in bands and performed at Battle of the Bands, but I've never studied music, and I couldn't read music. In those days the notes were colour-coded for me. It's made a big difference for me to learn to read the notes like everyone else.

Music theory has been a challenge. I had to work a lot harder than in my other courses to excel at it. At my college we have different teachers for different years of music theory, and one openly told us he has dyslexia, autism, and ADHD. He wants people to know that there are teachers like this. That was really cool for me and made a big impact on how I viewed myself as a student. Him sharing his story made me realize that I could do more things with my life. Perhaps I could become a Professor of Music as well.

Voice is my primary instrument, and I'm now learning piano, guitar, and drums which will further my career goals. It was wonderful that they accepted me on the course because of my audition tape, with these gaps in my experience. Everyone was patient as I muscled through the first term. I put in a lot of effort, saw tutors when I had to, made schoolwork my priority, and was very surprised to be ultimately awarded a scholarship.

Helping with Creativity

I think dyslexia helps with songwriting. It's part of what makes me creative, as I'm very in touch with my inner self. I'm able to make unique connections when using different writing themes and can memorize and recall sounds quickly. As well as this, past experiences in school have made me unafraid to be different and tell my story.

When I was in high school, I enjoyed sports and other activities such as creative writing. I think I could have enjoyed math and could possibly have been good at it as I'm quick to make connections once I have a basic understanding of the concepts. It would have helped to have had more support so that I would have grown to enjoy it without feeling pressure.

I think school has taught me a lot about perseverance and what it means to take care of yourself. In high school I studied hard and then burned out. In college you can't do that because there's always something to do. You have to find little ways to recover, so in the long term you'll sustain yourself. I plan better, having a more realistic idea of how long it might take to review my work.

Another change is that I often did my work in big chunks,

but now I know that a rhythm of study and breaks will help me stay focused.

Top Tip from Sarah: I've also improved in notetaking and study skills. Like many students, before college I didn't know how to take notes. I thought I had to write down everything. One of the teachers pulled something random from online and encouraged me to read it and tell him the main points. He said those were the notes I needed to take. That really helped.

I think I learn best when people explain things to me and I'm able to ask questions. It used to be intimidating and sometimes embarrassing to put up my hand in class because I wasn't sure how it would be received, but I've now started to ask a lot more. I find if something's on paper I can begin to overthink the material, as I'm used to checking written work multiple times. However, talking with someone or bouncing ideas off them brings me clarity, and helps me focus on the concepts.

Understanding Others

I think dyslexia might help me communicate because I pick up very quickly on the emotions of others. I can sense things from other people and can work out what's going on for them. This can be helpful but it's also distracting.

I'm grateful to my parents who have supported me to learn in whatever area I want, and to my teachers at school and at my college. At my college, we're blessed to have professors who really care about us and see us as individuals. In my wildest dreams – and believe me, mine were – there have been so many things I'd never thought I'd be able to do. Yet, at our college they see our potential. I'm constantly surprised by the goals they think I can reach. They've taught me that my experiences and how I saw myself in grade school* doesn't define who I am, or where I will go in life. As a result, I have more confidence in my future. I've learnt through their support that everyone has their own strengths and weaknesses. I am not going to let dyslexia define me. I am more than the box others have put me into. I've sometimes put myself into that box too. Instead, I'm going to carve the future I want for myself.

During this year I've begun to take time to understand that I'm human and everyone makes mistakes. In fact, the most successful people make the most mistakes because they're not afraid of failure. They don't give up, and they believe in their pursuits.

If you're at school now, as one of my professors says, 'Tell yourself it's easy'. I find the more I do that, the less I overthink things, and the more inspired I am to do the work. When we believe we can do things, they feel that bit easier. When you lose the fear of something, you're giving yourself a chance for it to become enjoyable.

It's so important to remember we all have our different strengths. If you don't excel in everything, it doesn't define you as a person. Sometimes your struggle might

* Grade school refers to school until age 18

have to do with the situation you're in. You may not have the support you need. But in the right headspace, there are a lot of different things that can contribute to your success, so try not to take your temporary difficulties to heart. In my final year in high school, I wrote in our grad book, 'One step at a time, one step at a time, one step at a time', and I think that is the answer.

Leaving school is exciting. Life gets better. There are so many more directions for you to take than you previously imagined. Take hold of your dreams, keep growing your abilities, fully embrace uncertainty, and discover what brings you joy. That choice will be yours.

> **"Everyone has their own strengths and weaknesses. I have learnt that I am not going to let dyslexia define me. Instead, I'm going to carve the future I want for myself."**

CHAPTER 3

Take Your Time

CONOR WHITE

HANNAH, 26, LONDON, ENGLAND

> **"It would be much better for people leaving school to know that they haven't just failed, that when they're older they can build on what they've achieved so far and find ways to get to where they want."**

When I left school at 16, I felt like a failure. That feeling overwhelmed everything else. All my friends were going on to sixth forms and university, and I hadn't passed any of my exams. Someone should have told me I could achieve later in my life, but no one did.

Everything I wanted was taken away from me, and my confidence went with it. I think it would be much better for people leaving school to know that they haven't just failed, that when they're older they can build on what they've achieved so far and find ways to get to where they want.

When I look back now, I think I didn't feel ready to be in a classroom and have all the pressures of passing exams and doing subjects I didn't enjoy. School could have moved me down into easier classes, and I was begging them to do this, but I know I could have worked harder too. I had no confidence in my writing or my ability to learn things. I remember opening my revision books and not having a clue, but I somehow didn't think I'd fail.

Once we finished school, I suffered because I lived for having my friends around me. They were my focal point and most of them had moved away. Despite this, I was determined to do all I could to build myself a successful life.

First I had to retake English and maths GCSEs* – maths three times because they forgot to tell me I'd passed it the second. I had Post-It notes everywhere, stuck all over our flat, trying to get the information into my brain.

From then on, I think I just learnt through the jobs I had.

When I was 17, I was given an apprenticeship in a local Montessori nursery for about three years, and I did my Level 3 exams in childcare when I was there. This was easier than school because it was more practical, and I was older. Then I left to become a nanny for one of the little boys who went there and his brother, which I absolutely loved. It was like being a full-time mum, but then handing back the kids every night. I knew them from six months old and the oldest is now ten. I still see them all the time.

Once both the boys started school and nursery, I had less responsibilities. That's when I began to think I needed a change.

I started working at a school for children with autism, most of them nonverbal, which was extremely challenging. This was a very, very tricky job and my approach was different to a lot of the others there. For the first time in my working life I clashed with my colleagues.

* GCSEs are qualifications taken in most of the UK at 16

I had only been there for six months when I made the decision to apply for university to study social work.

It was my friends who persuaded me to apply, just to see what would happen. I had never in a million years thought I would do this, and I felt sure I wouldn't be accepted anywhere, because I didn't have A Levels* and I heard that universities didn't like apprenticeships.

Top Tip from Hannah: I decided to help myself by building my experience, so I started volunteering for a charity, mentoring young people. I worked with a young boy who was autistic and had stopped going to school or leaving the house. I was the only person other than his mum he would speak to.

When I was given a place at university, I felt excited but anxious. I wasn't sure if I was academically smart enough, but I chose my course very carefully. I knew there was no 10,000-word dissertation at the end, so that was important. That would have put me right off.

Once I arrived at university I had to learn how to learn. That's not a skill I had ever had, but I enjoyed finding out how to write and how to gather research and use it. I'm still unconfident in these areas but I received a lot of help.

It was interesting to talk to my friends who went straight from school to uni. Some of them didn't go to lectures.

---

* A Levels are taken in most of the UK at 18

I think lots went to university because it's what's expected of you, and you go for the experience.

Going to university later on is very different. A lot of people on my course were older, some had kids. Social work was their second career. We all felt so grateful. None of us missed lectures. We supported each other. We knew we'd worked very hard to be there. Being around these people started to convince me that a degree was doable. It was the right timing.

I had left school feeling like that was the end of the world. My dyslexia diagnosis had come late, so I didn't quite believe it, but at university I was given proper help. They gave me a laptop with about 20 different programs, but I found this worse – just another thing I had to learn how to do. The thing I struggled with most was the words bouncing on the page when I'm writing essays. That's also a problem when I try to read.

What's so weird is that in my university essays, I did well. Last year, I got firsts in all of them. There's a very particular way you write at university, and it helps that I'm genuinely interested in the topic.

For the first two years of my degree, in the evenings, I worked at a residential care home for kids with disabilities. Again, I loved this. They were 16 to 25, which meant a big part of their life was obviously sex. So I wrote an essay about people with disabilities and sex, a kind of taboo subject that no one speaks about. I was given 82 per cent for that and it showed me how much easier I find it to write about things I feel strongly about.

Top Tip from Hannah: I've learnt how much time I need to write things. It takes me much longer than I would have thought. I just write a small amount a day. Having the right support helps me too. The lovely mum of a friend helped me read through my essays and she gave me a lot of confidence.

Now I am a youth justice social worker, working with kids who are in trouble with the police. I find the legal system interesting to learn about, and the level of intervention with young people is very satisfying. It feels so important to establish what happened to them in their lives that has taken them to the position they're in now.

I don't think anything I learnt at school helps me with my work now, except how to be around other people. I still struggle with reading and memory. I can read a page over and over again and then I think, 'What have I read?' It's to do with the language and understanding it. Reading out loud is my biggest fear. I even get overwhelmed reading children's books to my nephew. I think I'm going to make a mistake or say something wrong.

Gaining Confidence

I think the way I've built relationships in my working life has given me confidence, though I lack confidence generally. At meetings with other adults, I'm terrified, but as soon as they put me with a young person, I feel comfortable. I have worked out ways of dealing with situations when I'm uncomfortable – I need notes in some form to guide me in what I want to say.

I've always known that I like helping other people and working with anyone who needs extra support. I grew up seeing my mum taking care of my dad, who was unwell, and I've always had a caring instinct for others.

I'm caring in my friendships but my dyslexia affects them as well. Apparently I give no context when I talk, I'll just say something out of the blue and no one ever knows what I'm talking about, besides one of my friends who's also dyslexic.

If you're trying to support someone with dyslexia, I think you have to understand how they learn. It takes a very long time to get that understanding. Make sure you give them time to work things out. Having an assessment helped me, knowing the areas I struggle with, which I'd never known before. Dyslexia is so broad that without that knowledge how are you ever meant to help yourself?

I think it's a good idea to be vocal about having dyslexia at work, but then I've been lucky. Because I came to my new job through my university course, I had to say if I had any learning difficulties. My manager's dyslexic and she's created visual flow charts to explain the laws and the court system. Having the right support and being told I can have extra time to write a report has been so helpful.

I have had to learn ways to remember, taking notes, writing the meaning of a word next to it, rewording things in a language that I understand.

The most important thing anyone with dyslexia can do is find ways to believe in yourself. It's important not to settle for what you've got, if it's not all that you want. I was very content being a nanny, but that doesn't mean I was challenging myself. I wanted to prove that I could achieve my goals. And I have.

> **"Having an assessment helped me, knowing the areas I struggle with, which I'd never known before. Dyslexia is so broad that without that knowledge how are you ever meant to help yourself?"**

JAMIE, 21, GLASGOW, SCOTLAND

> **"Things didn't go well at first after school. I had nothing to go on to and felt like I was falling down a hole. My family and friends kept encouraging me and I found motivation from inside myself. I started thinking about what I really wanted to do."**

Life is much better since I left school. I've got a lot further than I thought I would. I've achieved so much more.

Things didn't go well for me at first. My careers adviser at school suggested I go to college to study cooking, and I tried this, but it wasn't for me. I left and I had nothing to go on to.

I thought everything would be downhill from there. I started not doing anything, just staying in all the time and not leaving the house. It felt like I was falling down a hole.

My family and friends kept encouraging me and I found motivation from inside of myself as well. I started thinking about what I really wanted to do.

I had been a volunteer for a group called DRC Generations for many years. This is an organization that works with young people so that they avoid drugs, alcohol, and tobacco misuse. They had helped me when I was at school, which was why I started volunteering with them, using what they'd taught me to help others. I knew how much I liked this sort of work and seeing the impact I can have. Even during my time at college, I never stopped the volunteering.

Making a Difference

This made me realize I wanted to help other young people, so I applied for a job as a youth and community worker, running youth groups and award schemes. I felt great when they gave it to me. Now I've moved on and I'm doing play work and after-school care. I love seeing the difference I can make with the children I'm working with.

At my lowest, I remembered the other thing I loved was entertainment and music. So, as well as applying for jobs in community work, I started setting up my own DJ business and getting that up and running. Now I do kids entertainment, with Disney costumes that I hire people to wear, and I do karaoke parties for adults. These also go down well. I want to build up this entertainment business so at some stage I can take a step back and know that other people are working out there for me.

I like both sides of the work I do, because they are so different and get me out and about, keeping me in touch with more people.

Dyslexia means I still struggle with some aspects of my work. Especially at the start of my community work we had to do quite a lot of risk assessments and other paperwork. Those were hard. I had to get other people to check them over before I showed them to the boss.

Setting up my website for my business and doing social media are difficult for me, as I try to make sure everything is spelt correctly. My spelling is a lot better than it used to be, but I still slip up.

Being dyslexic helps me with day-to-day work in ways that you wouldn't think. I put this down to the determination I developed from trying my best at school. With my caring work, I have this way of starting something and never stopping until I've finished. That's important to me.

I felt quite relieved when I left school, especially because they had given me support to get into college. My exams didn't feel like the easiest, but I managed to get through. I ended up doing better than I thought I would.

To be honest the volunteering I did feels even more important. I learnt so much while I was doing that, and I wouldn't be sitting where I am now if I hadn't. I would never have got the jobs I have without all this experience.

Top Tip from Jamie: One thing I learnt very young is to have good relationships with people, including everyone you work with. I find it easy to identify when people are struggling, partly because of all the training I've done now, including mental health training and dyslexia awareness, and having dyslexia myself.

Something else that helps is coming from a deprived area. When I was young, I got in with the wrong crowd. I've been in the shoes of the people I work with. It helps me relate to them and makes me want to help. They know I understand.

Support from family has been a big one for me, and my friends as well. Also the people I volunteered for at DRC have been great.

I think when you're helping someone with dyslexia, as well as complimenting them on what they do well and being positive about what they have achieved, don't be scared of telling them something they're doing wrong. If you don't tell them when it happens, it becomes harder to try to get out of the habit. If you know the first time what you've done, you can change it.

Top Tip from Jamie: Something else that's helpful is to practise interviews with them before their actual job interviews and double check their CVs or get someone else to.

For anyone still at school now and struggling with what they are doing, I can only say to stick at it. Try your hardest. That's all we can ever do. I had no idea when I was there where I was going to end up, but all along the way I did a lot to make sure things worked out well for me. Things go wrong or they go right. It either goes one way or the other. You need to put the effort in and try your best.

It was a fight to get to where I am, but I helped myself to stand out by volunteering while my friends were at home playing computer games. In the volunteering organizations, we all worked together. Those of us who have dyslexia all helped each other to get through.

We always have to keep open to learning. I learn all the time in my day-to-day life. Setting up a business was learning for me.

The most important thing I know is to have a goal for your future and keep at it. Do whatever you're interested in as this makes life much easier. Work can be hard, but it does get easier as time goes on with the more practice you have, and the creative side of dyslexia will help you in many different ways.

"For anyone still at school now and struggling with what they are doing, I can only say to stick at it. Try your hardest. That's all we can ever do. I had no idea when I was there where I was going to end up, but all along the way I did a lot to make sure things worked out well for me."

RYAN, 19, KILDARE, IRELAND

> "Dyslexia is not something you should be afraid of. I find a way to adapt to whatever I'm doing. It's about seeing yourself as your own person."

On the one-year course I'm doing now, I'm studying digital media, Photoshop, Illustrator, Adobe, web design, and photography. It's very interesting learning how to use the programs and finding out the different aspects used for advertising and graphic design.

After this I might carry on studying different media at university, but I also like working with my hands, mending cars and mechanical things, so I was thinking about going into something practical like that. I haven't made up my mind yet.

My skills that come from dyslexia could help with both of these pathways. I always feel dyslexia is not a bad thing. It's not something you should be afraid of. I almost use it as a positive and I find a way to adapt to whatever I'm doing. It's about seeing yourself as your own person.

Right now, my out-of-the-box thinking makes a difference to what I'm doing. Last Monday I was out on a photoshoot with one of the college researchers who was studying ancient woodlands in Ireland. We had to go into the woods and take photos and I was interviewing him, as well as taking shots with drones. I was showing the different angles we could use for the photos and the video that might look better, and the researcher took my ideas into account.

Luckily with the course I'm on there's no note taking. Everything is on the computer screen. At college we have different equipment to help you read. You can write on a board, then tap it with a pen and it plays back what you've written down.

The worst thing for me now is procrastination. This happens mainly at the start of a project. I found that in school you could just leave all the work and stress there, but in college you bring your work home and it doesn't feel like you're getting much of a break.

When I left school, I was kind of relieved. I just felt that school was done. I could move on to my next chapter and get down to what I wanted to do in life. There was a sort of freedom. I still feel that now. In college I can be more myself and study what I want to. There's such a choice. In school there were a few things I liked but I've always been very bad at maths and some bits of the English classes. Languages weren't great either. I'm trying to think about it now, but everything I learnt about in school has gone out of my head.

I was sad to leave the memories and the friends I'd made in school but I'm fortunate that I live in the same town, so I see a lot of people that were in school with me around the place.

One good thing about school and college is that in both cases it was all continuous assessment and no exams.

This was because at school I was doing what's called the Leaving Certificate Applied in Ireland. I don't like the pressure of exams, and I can manage projects more easily. I think all schools should offer the choice of continuous assessment to people who aren't good at exams. This can help you prepare for college as well.

Help from Others

I've received a lot of help, from my mum and dad, and my school and college. School had a whole programme of extra classes for people with learning difficulties. It's so important for people supporting you to be patient. Then we will get there in the end – especially if you explain things in more than one way.

> **Top Tip from Ryan:** I find all the time that if someone tells me something, I say, 'Can you give me an example?', or 'What would you do differently?' I try to look at things from different angles, instead of just the one.

One great thing about my course now is that I'm doing work experience at the same time. I think school helped me develop the confidence and people skills to do this. In Ireland we can do what's called a transition year and I learnt on that to stretch myself out of my comfort zone, especially when I had to do presentations about a subject in front of a lot of people my age. Something else that was useful was the way they included real life in maths lessons. We had to make a business plan and buy products and sell them and work out what kind of profit we were going to make. That helped maths make much more sense and we learnt how useful it could be.

I feel like 20 per cent of everything I've learnt has been in school. The rest has been outside of school, by doing things like watching people, seeing how they react, seeing their body language, and stuff like that.

If I put myself through a stressful situation, like my driving test, the next time I do it, all the things that would have been stressful the first time kind of get easier. You get stronger as a person by pushing yourself like that.

Dog with a Bone

Sometimes there's banter here and there with my friends about dyslexia, but we would never exclude each other because of something like this. I would never take anything they said to heart. When I text, I get things wrong but Autocorrect helps. I don't do a lot of social media, but I don't think dyslexia would affect it that much as I mainly take photos. My timekeeping is quite bad, but when there's something I want to do, my dad says I'm like a dog with a bone. If I'm keen, I'll be there.

Dyslexia can hold me back. My handwriting is horrible. I remember when I was working in a bar, it was annoying to write down orders and stuff like that. I always have a bit of stress with going on tills – I can't calculate people's bills as fast as other people can. I found if my manager told me to do something I wouldn't process the instructions as quickly as my friends. If I'm asked to do more than one thing I will forget one of them. Definitely.

> **Top Tip from Ryan:** In a workplace, if you don't know what to do, having friends there is useful. This means that rather than a boss explaining something to you, you can have your colleagues explaining it to you. Someone your own age is more likely to talk to you in a way that you understand.

I can make up my mind after this year what I want to do. Even if I decide to do a bachelor's degree, I will have freedom after that. I definitely want to travel to different places and see different types of culture. I think I would learn a lot by doing that.

Everyone should remember that school doesn't last forever. Don't wish the years away, because sometimes I still wish I was back there with the friends I made, not having the worries of making a decision about which direction to take now and thinking about getting a job in the future and trying to make a living. With all parts of our lives there are things we gain and things we are happy to leave behind.

> **"Everyone should remember that school doesn't last forever. Don't wish the years away, because sometimes I still wish I was back there with the friends I made, not having the worries of making a decision about which direction to take now."**

RHOMI, 26, LONDON, ENGLAND

> "Learning has a balancing scale. If one area of your life is down, then the other is high up. That's why running businesses comes so naturally to me, as a practical person."

When I was at university I was so stressed with the workload, I found myself itching my hair a lot. My scalp was feeling unbearable. One day I woke up and realized I was losing hair from the anxiety I felt about my assignments. I thought I had no choice. I ended up doing a 'big chop' and shaving off all my hair.

After a while I thought, 'OK, I'm going to start to grow my hair back healthily'. That's when I began to research natural haircare products, so my new hair would be in the best possible condition. I started making my own and using them. People saw that my hair was growing a lot and looking strong, and they wanted that for themselves. That's when my business idea came to me.

My products are quite different from anything else out there on the market. Most hair products are full of chemicals. Mine are made by me in my kitchen at home. They work and I've seen the results. I see them every morning in the mirror! The products are for black women but also suit hair from other cultures.

I also have experiences in running other businesses. My first was selling cakes. I learnt to bake using YouTube videos: birthday cakes, wedding cakes, all sorts of cakes, made in my own home from scratch. After that I set up a hair braiding business. That was useful too.

> **Top Tip from Rhomi:** To help with the business, I took some free adult courses at City & Islington College which is local to me. One was in website design, which means I don't have to pay anyone else to set up my website. Others were in business administration and business marketing. They have all been great.

When I was at school, things felt much more difficult for me. I'm not going to say I was the best-behaved student – I think that was because I found classroom learning so hard, though school did teach me the importance of being a moral and honest person.

Helping Myself

Something else I learnt at school was to find ways to help myself. Using my practical side, I invented revision methods that worked for me.

> **Top Tip from Rhomi:** One talent of mine is singing, and when I couldn't remember something, I made up a song about that subject. I just taught one of my science songs to my little brother before he took his science exam and he said it helped him as well.

When I did put in the work, sometimes I saw the results of it, but there were times when I did the best I could and still didn't achieve the grades.

When I left I felt OK because I had my support network around me to encourage me. I went to college to do a course in Health and Social Care. The assignments were challenging but I was able to overcome this.

Coming from an African background, you can be seen as stupid if you don't go to university, so I decided to go, but this was always a fallback position for me, in case my businesses didn't work out.

University felt quite scary. I was doing a degree in nursing, and when it came to writing assignments, I struggled to understand what was required and I kept failing. I knew this was because of dyslexia. It was like I knew what I needed to do, but my brain just didn't. I always understood the context and I had the information I needed, but the way I was placing all my words wasn't flowing correctly. The lecturers would mark the work and say the structure wasn't right. I was saying, 'It looks right to me'. I understood what I was trying to say but they couldn't make sense of it. I had to get friends and family to help me and look over my work. Those were the only times where I would pass.

I failed two of my years and had to retake them, so it took me five years to do a three-year degree.

Once I passed, I found I was scared to do the job. When you first graduate you are monitored by professional nursing staff, to help you along the way. However, there comes a time when that stops and you're on your own. I was so frightened I'd make a mistake, like forgetting to give someone their medication. When I was working on a shift, a doctor might tell me something and I wouldn't remember what they said. I decided to walk around with a sheet of paper to write everything on, but that felt silly. I worried my memory would let me down.

Luckily nursing was always only my backup plan. I always wanted to be a businesswoman. I find it quite interesting that learning has a balancing scale. If one area of your life is down, then the other is high up. That's why running businesses comes so naturally to me, as a practical person. I think being practical is partly down to my dyslexia, but it's also the way I was brought up as my parents are both hands-on people.

I think dyslexia may affect my friendships. I must communicate differently. I worry that my words won't flow properly or that I'll lose my train of thought. If people are having a debate or a discussion, I zone out. There are too many words to process. It's like I'm being required to use an area of my brain that I can't.

Great Support

Despite this, I've had great support, from my fiancé, my friends, and my sister. My parents don't want me to 'claim' I have dyslexia, even if the tests have come back saying I have. They want me to be secretive about it. It's a cultural thing.

I tell myself that everyone has a problem, whether they've hidden it or haven't hidden it. Everyone is struggling with something. No one should be afraid to ask for help and someone will be willing to help you. Ask, ask, ask, ask, ask.

If you want to support someone with dyslexia, be patient with them. The way they understand information is different to the way you do. Eventually they will get there. I've had to fight my way through life, while knowing deep inside that I am a practical person and that's what will lead me to success. The same is true of anyone reading this. Set your mind on doing something and you will get there.

"I tell myself that everyone has a problem, whether they've hidden it or haven't hidden it. Everyone is struggling with something. No one should be afraid to ask for help and someone will be willing to help you. Ask, ask, ask, ask, ask."

HALLE LEARMOUTH
'NO MATTER WHAT, GIVEN TIME YOU WILL FLOURISH'
INSTAGRAM: BADLY.DRAWN.ART | ARTSTATION: BADLYDRAWNART

PATRICK, 24, CHRISTCHURCH, NEW ZEALAND

> "Life after school has been rewarding in some ways and challenging in others. The older I get, the more I understand that dyslexia isn't a thing that becomes super easy and manageable when you become an adult."

Right now, I feel as if I'm still finding my footing in adult life, but I've learnt a lot along the way. These are valuable lessons that will help me in the future.

Life after school has been rewarding in some ways and challenging in others. I think the older I get, the more I understand that dyslexia isn't a thing that becomes super easy and manageable when you become an adult. It's something you've always got to manoeuvre around.

Looking back, high school was good. The support I had there was probably some of the best I've received. There are things that could have been done better, and sometimes I was pushed to do schoolwork that felt overwhelming. I was kept from things that I wanted to do, based purely on the school not having the resources to create a learning support programme for the lesson.

I used to feel a lot of shame when I was younger for having a support aid or having extra time. My peers would be going, 'You've only got these grades because you've got a support person', or 'Oh, you're stupid because you've got a support aid'. As if I didn't do any work!

That left me thinking I needed to work on my own, but the older I've got, the more I've realized that no one does anything on their own. Everyone's getting support somewhere. This has been part of my growing up – there are things that you're just not going to know how to do and that's OK.

At school I was a very determined person, but when I left, I felt beyond lost. The structure and the safety net that I had were gone. I struggled entering the workforce and not having a support worker or an exam to work towards. It's something I think I still struggle with sometimes.

For a long time, I wanted to be an actor, and I tried to get into drama school. It just didn't work out. There's a culture issue in New Zealand that goes if you're not the best at something, why would you do it? There's also what we call 'crossing cringe mountain'. This is when you're not good at something but you're putting your whole self into it, and it's embarrassing to watch, but you have to do it to improve, and we all have to have the courage to put ourselves out there.

Then I worked in a warehouse putting windshields in boxes for eight hours a day. I did this as well as anyone, but I find it will always take me just a little bit longer to learn any skill. It was trial and error, until I found my way of doing it right.

Afterwards I did Camp America and worked as a camp

counsellor, which was uplifting and fun. I loved working with young people. I also enjoyed being a lifeguard there, and just being able to see the change in the kids through one single summer. It wasn't a teaching role, it was more like being an older brother, giving them a little guidance when they needed it.

I taught swimming, and the teachers there were saying I should become a teacher, but I don't know how I would do in a classroom space. I get overwhelmed with noise and recede into myself, so I'm not sure I would do my best.

Then I took my degree in broadcasting and communications, which is pretty cool, especially as I was told I wouldn't pass high school. After this I worked in the radio industry for six months. I thought this was going to be creative and uplifting but I quickly learnt that it was commercialized and corporate and not for me.

Overall I think my degree taught me valuable skills, and I can transfer them to another industry if I need to.

I think what I learnt at university helped me more than what I learnt at high school. The structure of essays we learnt at school was nothing like what we learnt at university. When I started university, I was like, 'This is like *Saving Private Ryan*. Thrown in with no knowledge. Not helpful at all.'

My partner, Liam, has been a super help and so has my best friend. One is an English major and one is a lawyer, and they gave me the full teacher feedback on my essays of, 'This doesn't make sense', and 'What do you mean by this?' The whole red underline and all that stuff. I need that just to feel confident in what I am doing.

I need someone to say, 'You're going in the right direction. You're doing good'. Without that I would be thinking, 'I'm an idiot who doesn't know how to do anything'.

I've just gotten a job at a retail store. I'm grateful for that because I've had some dyslexic issues. I had my phone number wrong on my CV for six months. That felt so avoidable, but it's all a learning opportunity.

Dyslexia does help me. My brain pieces together information from a different viewpoint. At one point I was an intern and working as a creative writer in radio for advertisements. When I was in a brainstorming session, I would always be coming up with things: 'Maybe we should try like this. Maybe this can be different'.

My team was supportive about my dyslexia, proofreading my scripts before we submitted them to clients. Mind you, I would only tell people I have dyslexia after I've got a job. People love a good reason not to hire somebody.

I enjoyed the job and solving problems for clients, being able to come up with creative solutions about things that they need. I learnt that most people don't want to do anything weird or a bit different. It would be like, 'I don't want to do that as it's not what the other real estate agent or the other construction company did'.

The real show of character is how you deal with things

that go wrong. If you send an email out that's spelt incorrectly, are you then sending the client a new, updated, correct version? Or are you still freaking out? These are things I still struggle with.

Top Tip from Patrick: I've learnt some useful lessons everywhere. School taught me I can't concentrate if my phone is anywhere near me. If I get a notification, I can be distracted for hours. University taught me you have to do your best and not expect things to go right all the time.

I think what's taught me the most in life is failing. I know that sounds like such a Miss America Pageant thing to say, but I feel like that's true. I feel like I've failed far more than I've succeeded with things I've tried to do. It may be a bit more painful, but the lesson got learnt. You have to swallow it and move on. Figure out what you're going to do and try again.

I've learnt valuable skills from being in situations where I'm unsure of myself. Being comfortable enough to ask members of my support network for help is vital. That's something that took me a long time to do but now I can't imagine being without it.

Horrific Texts

I would say dyslexia is like a mild inconvenience 70 per cent of the time. But that other 30 per cent there are some good nuggets in there. I wouldn't trade that: it's the way I interact with the world. Mind you, with my friends, I'm horrific at sending messages. I'm a terrible responder, awful at being like 'Yeah, let's hang out in three weeks' and not remembering that I've said that.

My mum has always been my number one person supporting me, in the trenches when I was a kid, advocating for me. As I've gotten older, my partner has stepped up at being someone I can rely on.

Supporting someone with dyslexia is a lot about patience. For a neurotypical person this can be quite frustrating – why wouldn't you just rote learn your times tables or whatever it is? Having a bit of grace and understanding that some brains don't work the same as yours is what it takes. We are trying, it just takes time.

Some people with dyslexia seem to have grown into their adult selves. I can still get stuck, telling myself I'm dumb and not good at things, which is just not true. Despite this, hands down, life is better after school. That's my message. I'm not quite on the right path yet, but once you stop looking to your left and right and keep your eyes on what you're achieving and what you want, that's when things are easier.

"My mum has always been my number one person supporting me, in the trenches when I was a kid, advocating for me. As I've gotten older, my partner has stepped up at being someone I can rely on."

GEORGE, 23, LONDON, ENGLAND

> **“A lot of what I’ve learnt over the years has come from my experiences in life. When I talked my way into university, that’s when the penny dropped that there are multiple ways to succeed. Not everyone does it the same way.”**

Leaving secondary school wasn’t the easiest time for me. I left at 18 with two A Levels, in Geography and Politics, knowing universities want you to have three. I had this big question hanging over me: ‘What’s next?’

Then I saw there was a degree at London South Bank University to study property management and building surveying. I’m interested in property management, and after half an hour on the phone persuading a very nice lady in admissions, she agreed to give me a place. I was very lucky, but I can waffle, which is one of my strengths.

I ended up doing pretty decently in my first year. Then I visited a friend in Oxford, a very clever guy. I was in Oxford for the first time, surrounded by the beautiful buildings and all these smart people. I thought it would be great if I could go there one day, to prove to myself that I’m not stupid, after having been completely average or below average at school for all those years.

I started looking at Oxford degrees. No surprise that you needed top marks in everything. Four A Stars, all the GCSEs. Then I realized that for a master's degree they don't take A Levels into account.

I decided that was my benchmark. I wanted to make a point to myself, to be where all the smart kids were, after feeling like one of the dumbest in the class.

Switching My Course

I also decided to switch my degree. I dropped out of South Bank after my first year and applied to universities for Law. Because I'd done well in that year, I managed to get a place in Cardiff. There I did decently, and while I didn't get into Oxford to do a master's degree afterwards, I did get into UCL in London, another top university.

I now have a straight Law degree and I'm doing a master's degree in International Commercial Law. I've worked really hard, but I feel it's luck that it's all ended up working out. It just kind of happened. I am proud of myself, but I didn't achieve my goal of getting into Oxford and I guess the truth is I don't feel very different from how I did back in school.

A lot of studying for law is rote reading and intensive writing. I know this takes me a lot longer than other people. I've had to get good at becoming organized in my calendar and knowing what's happening at all times.

Although I struggle with it, time management is very helpful. It brings order to the day. Something difficult for me is being realistic about how long things are going to take me, especially when I compare myself to my nondyslexic friends. I ask them how much they've done today. They've done X, Y, and Z and I've done half of X.

Sometimes I struggle to focus. Today I got to the library at 9.30 am and next time I looked it was somehow 10.30 am. I had been making calls for the business I'm starting this year: an online business selling shirts and kits for volleyball teams.

I've got the website sorted and the social media to sell through the website. I've seen the freedom that running a business has brought my family and I might want that for myself. It's not ideal, but when you're studying, other stuff does seem much more interesting.

> **Top Tip from George:** I tend to see things a lot in black and white, which might be down to my dyslexia. Before I decided which modules to take here, I made a big Excel sheet. All I cared about was whether the exams were in person, or online, or coursework. Everything that was in person, I deleted. I didn't care how interesting it was, I just knew I would do badly. It's about making smarter choices. It's knowing yourself and making the right decisions for you.

My mother's an immigrant from Brazil and my dad is a Greek Cypriot. They have both done exceptionally well, but I didn't heed their advice about my schooling, or the advice my teachers gave, so I felt I was making my way on my own.

In school I was quite decent in maths, but other subjects were almost a lost cause. I was in very low sets, and I remember thinking, 'Am I really this bad?'

I feel like a lot of what I've learnt over the years has come from my experiences in life. When I talked my way into South Bank, that's when the penny dropped that there are multiple ways to succeed. Not everyone does it the same way.

A girlfriend I had in Oxford was the smartest person I knew. We used to argue about things, and she would say, 'Logically what you're saying doesn't work'. She taught me so much about how to formulate arguments and how to express myself. She helped me see I had critical thinking skills. I realized I must have a half decent brain.

Another thing that helped me was going to my dyslexia tutors, Seth and Delia. This is one thing my parents got right. My tutors created a relationship where I felt very comfortable. It wasn't just, 'Come in, sit down, here's some maths, now go away'. I learnt lots of things from them that helped me get through school.

> **Top Tip from George:** Something else that taught me a lot was feeling quite lonely at secondary school. That pushed me to not be lonely now. I can see now how negative things can be positive in the end, and push you forwards.

Some of the things we learn at school are useful. They mean we're not completely stupid when we leave. For example, I can work out a percentage. I don't use biology all the time, but I understand how a vaccine works. I think being rounded in what you know is important. Specializing is obsolete now. If you're an expert in building a particular car and then a machine comes along to do it, you're not needed any more. If you know about the whole process, a lot of what you know can be used in other places.

The people you surround yourself with are what's most important. I would put everything I've achieved down to the people around me: Seth and Delia, my ex at Oxford, my mum and dad, and friends.

If you're trying to support someone with dyslexia, the motivation has to come from them. I remember learning the difference between two and to and there and their. I didn't care at the time, but because I did it, things have become easier. Having said that, some of this has to be forced because kids will never want to do this stuff. Even now my spelling is terrible, and I don't try to hide it. Especially in law, you get a lot of fancy language, and I have a list of words I don't know. I've been doing the list for years now. It goes on and on and on.

Something I would advise people with dyslexia to consider is apprenticeships. One of my friends from school did a plumbing apprenticeship. He's my age now and he has a house with a mortgage. He's made a hell of a lot more money than I have at this point. It would have suited me well because I'm very practical, but I just didn't want to be seen as the 'dumb kid'. Looking at things realistically I don't think most people need to go to university to do a good job. Even with law there are apprenticeships. You can work for a firm, and they teach you there, which is a lot more valuable.

Life has taught me that just because you're not good at something doesn't mean you can't be good at it later. Talent doesn't beat hard work, which is what I've had to do. Dyslexia does mean that we are different, and we work in different ways, but I never imagined doing as well as I have. When I was taking two A Levels this was unheard of in my school. It was just so bad. Now I'm doing a master's at UCL.

Options are especially important for someone with dyslexia because our brains aren't linear. They don't work in a straight line. I think my brain has the habit of bouncing around. I'm interested in something and then I think there's nothing worse than what I'm doing.

Despite this, if you haven't got the qualifications, it's a helpless feeling. I wanted to go to university, and I found a way, but it wasn't straightforward. I should feel proud, but I also feel that I haven't done anything yet. This is just the beginning.

"Life has taught me that just because you're not good at something doesn't mean you can't be good at it later. Talent doesn't beat hard work, which is what I've had to do. Dyslexia does mean that we are different, and we work in different ways, but I never imagined doing as well as I have."

CHAPTER 4

Find Ways to Help Yourself

MAX, 24, BAY OF PLENTY, NEW ZEALAND

“Because I was dyslexic, I struggled to connect with what was being taught at school. I wasn’t quite getting it in the way everyone else was. I stopped going and did pretty much all my high school years at home, using an online school programme. This was better for me. It meant I could work at my own pace. It freed up a lot more time to do stuff that I was actually interested in.”

Every day I think about how almost pointless school was. I feel like it was a waste of time, a way of wasting my life. There’s a lot that doesn’t get taught, from basic life skills like how to open a bank account, to more career-focused subjects. If someone tends to lean towards a particular line of work, why wouldn’t you encourage that?

I think because I was dyslexic, I struggled to connect with what was being taught. I wasn’t quite getting it in the way everyone else was.

Because of this, I stopped going to school and did pretty much all my high school years at home, using an online school programme. This was better for me. It meant I could work at my own pace. It freed up a lot more time to do stuff that I was actually interested in. I’ve gotten a lot of fruit from that.

I think by a pretty young age I had figured out what I was

good at, and my path was pretty clear from there. While I did my schoolwork at home, I worked part-time as a mechanical engineer. I heard of a company that had a vacancy caused by an injury to one of the team members, and they needed someone to fill in.

Apprenticeship

After school I did an apprenticeship with very similar work to what I was doing throughout high school. I had to complete booklets and get them signed off as proof that I had the knowledge to complete jobs safely. This was very technical and specific. I could work at my own pace, but this could still be challenging sometimes when you have a big block of words and it's technical information and you need to fully understand it. It could take me quite a while to get through that stuff.

Now I have my first level qualification in automotive engineering, and I'm doing an agricultural equipment level qualification as well. I have led a small team of engineers and that's pretty cool.

I don't know what it is I like so much about engineering, but I just get it. It makes sense to me. I always thought I was good at spatial things and that helps a lot with the work I do. We designed a product not too long ago and I was involved in the process. It felt like all those skills I have came into use.

Because I had already started work while I was doing my schooling, carrying on in the workplace was quite organic.

I'm at a different company now and I feel like my career is progressing well.

In all my education I feel like there have been a couple of things that have been helpful, but all of that stuff was learnt in my high school years through correspondence courses when I was teaching myself. I was able to chase down information independently that was helpful to me, like Pythagoras' theorem and a lot of geometry. Stuff that I use every day. I had time to dive into details that I didn't understand at the time, but I could find the information and learn about it.

When it came to English, spelling, and reading, I still struggle quite a bit with that. At work we have to type out jobs when we complete them, so everyone knows where things stand. I'm not the only one there who isn't very good at spelling or punctuation. It seems there are two types of bad handwriting – doctors' and mechanics' – so I manage to get away scot-free there. It's what people expect.

Despite this, I feel like dyslexia gives you access to another side of your brain and gives you ideas that other people can't quite see at the time. It's just another way to look at things. With problem solving especially, it seems to be quite helpful.

> **Top Tip from Max:** If there's a way that something's always been done, dyslexia means you can see a different way to do it that works just as well and could be faster. Your vision isn't limited by what's already in place.

There are times when work can be difficult, as a result of dyslexia. Maths in general, excluding geometry, can be quite tricky. Also, misspelling things all the time is hard, and it makes it hard for people to understand what I'm trying to say. These are mostly little trip-ups, nothing major.

I learnt just last week that disc is spelt with a C, not a K. That was quite an eye opener!

I still struggle with reading. I used to read quite a lot. Now I haven't done it in quite a while, and I can't read as well as I used to. The issue for me is reading big blocks of words. I can't quite understand what I'm reading even though it's very plain English and right in front of me.

I don't let this hold me back. My attitude to life is that if you're interested in something, don't be afraid to learn about it and chase it as best you can. I'm a detail-orientated person, but when it comes to seeing the bigger picture, I felt like I always knew where I was headed. It's a passion for what I do that drove me towards where I was going.

Dyslexia doesn't affect my friendships or relationships in that here in New Zealand it's a little bit more widely known, so people understand it better. I think it's a lot less polarizing. My texting is riddled with spelling mistakes and has no punctuation, but I get by. Even though I left school very young, I still have some pretty close friends outside of school that I've known for a very long time. We've sort of been friends forever, so I don't feel I lost anything.

When I think back to who has helped me, I would say definitely Mum. She was the one who found out quite early on that I was dyslexic, who brought up information that showed I wasn't weird, just that my mind works differently. If she hadn't done that it would have been a lot longer before I realized it wasn't just that I didn't understand my schoolwork. I would have been a much less confident person. The confidence I have comes from the fact that I've been well supported.

Anyone supporting someone with dyslexia, I think their messages should be along the same lines. It's not weird, it's just something different. And different isn't bad, it's just not the same as everyone else.

> **Top Tip from Max:** I think it's helpful if people know early on that you're struggling with what can seem like basic things. I know in New Zealand there's quite a lot of support for dyslexia. So readers/writers are things that you can ask for. Being upfront has been beneficial for me. If you feel you've reached a roadblock, I've found that a lot of people are OK with helping. Schoolwork will always be more difficult. You can struggle through it by yourself, and you might find ways to get around it, but it is OK to ask for help.

Life is so much better after school. I've already decided I'm going to stay in the same industry and see how far I can take it. I have a lot to look forward to.

"My attitude to life is that if you're interested in something, don't be afraid to learn about it and chase it as best you can. I'm a detail-orientated person, but when it comes to seeing the bigger picture, I felt like I always knew where I was headed. It's a passion for what I do that drove me towards where I was going."

ZOE-JANE, 25, BIRMINGHAM, ENGLAND

> “We feel we need to prove ourselves, and it’s so important that we also help others build the future that’s right for them, using their skills and abilities, while gaining the support they need.”

Dyslexia is difficult, and if you’re someone like me who is a woman of colour, or comes from a poorer area, these things can be against us too. That’s why I always want to pass on what I’ve learnt to others. I want to show there’s light at the end of the tunnel for those on a journey that’s not always easy.

We feel we need to prove ourselves, and it’s so important that we also help others build the future that’s right for them, using their skills and abilities, while gaining the support they need.

When I was at school, my life was confusing. I was fortunate in that I was screened in Year 6, when I was about 11, when a supply teacher noticed I was dyslexic. This meant in secondary school, college, and uni, I had the extra support, the extra time, and the space away from the main hall to take my exams. I always wonder what life could have been like if I hadn’t been assessed.

There was something empowering knowing that there was a reason why things weren’t that good for me in school. On the other hand, no one had explained why my working memory was terrible or why my spelling

was the way it was. I had the label of dyslexia but no understanding about what it meant.

At secondary school I was able to mask my difficulties, and my grades weren't too terrible until I reached Year 10. Then things went downhill. When I left I mostly felt relieved, having felt misunderstood by a lot of teachers and pupils, though I had bittersweet times of missing the buzz you get from talking to everyone.

Sport Was My Release

College felt like a fresh start. There I studied sport, which was my release. I had always felt it was the only thing I was good at. It was what my dyslexic brain understood.

Sport has been a part of my life since I started dancing when I was three. I was a child with way too much energy, and I just enjoyed feeling free. I didn't need to wear what felt like a mask to try to fit in with everyone else. On the sporting field I was just me. My so-called disability became a massive ability.

I hadn't expected to go to uni, but because I excelled at college, I retook my maths and applied to study Sports Therapy.

I found that the further up in education you go, the more support you get with dyslexia, which is quite unfair, because not everyone gets to climb that ladder.

My biggest assets with being dyslexic are pattern

recognition and creativity. So when I was playing sports, and my main sport was netball, I found it easy to pick up on what the other players would do. I saw they repeated the same patterns over and over again. I tried to tell my teammates, 'Listen, there's a pattern. I can see it'. At first people thought I was crazy. Then they understood that maybe I was right. What I was saying made sense.

My creativity helped too. No matter what sport it was, I'd always put my own spin on it. This was the first time my dyslexia was seen as a good thing. It wasn't just 'you can't spell very well', or 'why are you daydreaming?'

After a while the stereotypes came back in and dyslexia was more of a burden. When I played sport and said that I was dyslexic, some people were saying, 'You're not gonna be spelling. What has that to do with it?' I explained it wasn't just spelling; it was working memory. I needed time to process information. Short breaks weren't enough time for me.

I think they just didn't understand and thought I was just a bit slow.

I felt I wasn't understood or heard, because everyone just thinks dyslexia is reading and writing. If only they had taken their time, they could have understood how to harness my dyslexia for everything it could have given them. There are so many amazing athletes who are neurodivergent.

As I got older, I found things harder; my mask had slipped. Although this could be annoying, it also meant I had started to be authentically myself, which I was grateful for. It took a lot of pressure off me. I decided to do my own research about what dyslexia was.

Giving Back

I began working as a sports therapist and I noticed how much I enjoyed talking to young people about their lives. We started discussing CVs and careers. Before I knew it, I was a sports therapist and a careers advisor at the basketball club I was helping at. This felt so random, but I enjoyed being able to give back to young people who are feeling confused and don't know where to get support.

This has led me to where I am now. I'm an education and skills team leader for a sports organization, working with 16–29-year-olds. I help them get into work or ready for work. I create content, like writing CVs, and I do public speaking. I look at how the young people I work with communicate and what their life skills are. We work on how they get their voices heard. We do mock interviews. A lot of them didn't have the best time at school - many are neurodivergent without the means to get a diagnosis.

The more I researched about dyslexia, the more I started posting about it on my socials. Then I realized there are a lot of people who don't know about it. Since then, it's been part of my personal journey and it's great to help others at the same time. I have also realized that I may have come from a single parent family and faced difficulties growing up, but I was fortunate to come from a supportive background and have a supportive network.

A lot of people don't, whether that's because of a cultural lack of acceptance or things just not working at home.

> **Top Tip from Zoe-Jane:** I realize now that school wasn't able to teach me much when it came to the curriculum, but it did teach me about structure, to be somewhere when I need to be there. It gave me the foundation of being able to organize my time well, in manageable sections, because that is what the school day is like.

I've learnt other lessons through everything I've done. I learn through hands-on stuff and through developing my own projects. I learn through being able to talk to people. School is certainly not the only place you learn. There are an endless number of resources available to us. As you get older you come to understand that learning can be from anywhere and from anyone. It can be from kids who are younger than you and from people who are older than you. I love watching a good YouTube video and hearing someone explain things, though I put them on double the speed because my brain is strange like that. I learn well by hearing different people explain things in different ways.

I always recommend people try different ways of learning. At university I bought a full-sized skeleton so I could pass my anatomy exam. Everyone thought I was crazy. My mum cursed me because it took up so much space in her house, but that was my way of learning. Who cares if something's weird if it helps you take in information?

Failure Helps You Succeed

I think self-education is key. Work out how you get the best out of yourself. Remember that failure is not a bad thing, and that it helps you succeed in the end. It makes you a stronger person and helps you accept yourself. With me I still have bad days with my dyslexia, and that's normal. It's so bad sometimes I can forget I've had a conversation with a friend, and they're like, 'You know, you've already said this.' Then I look like the friend who isn't listening or doesn't care, which is the opposite of how I feel. I care dearly for my friends. It's just my working memory is really bad.

I know there are friends who have fallen out with me because when I type a message I am so direct. That's why I prefer voice notes so you can hear the tone of what I'm saying. When I type I sound like a moody person. I wonder if when you're dyslexic you fear being misunderstood more than other people do.

On the other hand, I love social media. I've been able to connect with loads of people. I'm quite candid about dyslexia and I say it as it is. I want to get the message across that it's normal. My spelling is terrible, so I try to get what I write pre-read by my partner if he's around, but I put something out a while ago, and I'd written dairy instead of diary. Who wants to read dairy instead of diary? I tell myself I have a dyslexic page. I've stated I'm dyslexic, so that means you are going to see spelling mistakes and it's not the end of the world if you can get what I'm saying.

Top Tip from Zoe-Jane: I tell the young people I work with that I'm dyslexic, and if I say anything wrong let it go, but if you think it's bad, please let me know. That gets a chuckle out of them, and it also gives them permission to know that it's OK to make mistakes.

That kind of positive message is so important. I had that from my mum. She gave me the confidence to keep pushing. I pushed throughout school. My results weren't always great, but she never held that against me. She was the most supportive person.

She taught me that being patient and open-minded is key. It's not always easy and we can get frustrated. If you have dyslexia you go through school and even through work sometimes not feeling accepted, but we can still be ourselves.

No one should have to struggle alone. Find something that brings you happiness, whether it's a hobby or something else to put your frustrated energy into. Most importantly, find that supportive network, whether it's through school, through friends, through family, and if you truly feel like there isn't anybody, have a look online for supportive groups, or hotlines, because there are people to talk to.

Then find a job that you enjoy. Be open-minded about your future choices and remember failure will teach you so much, so don't fear it. Look for employers who support you, don't just take any job you're forced to do. I know as a manager how much I can help those in my organization who are neurodivergent, changing the contents of what we produce, making the writing bigger, using more pictures in our materials. It's not difficult.

Most of all, ask for help if you need it. You may fear people will judge you, but never forget there are other people everywhere going through exactly the same as we are.

> **"As you get older you come to understand that learning can be from anywhere and from anyone. It can be from kids who are younger than you and from people who are older than you. I love watching a good YouTube video and hearing someone explain things."**

PO, 18, VICTORIA, AUSTRALIA

"My plan when I leave here is to study industrial design in automotive, at the university right next to where I am now. I'm interested in designing stuff and I'm interested in cars and motorbikes and all the graphic design that comes behind them."

At times at school, I felt as if I was the only one who couldn't cope. I couldn't deal with the work I was being given and I was being bullied.

I thought things would keep on getting worse, but then I found out how important it is for me to speak out about how I felt. By telling people, I developed a support system and managed to get help. That has made all the difference.

At 16, I left school to go to secondary college. My plan when I leave here is to study industrial design in automotive, at the university right next to where I am now. I'm interested in designing stuff and I'm interested in cars and motorbikes and all the graphic design that comes behind them.

Where I am now it's more grown up than school. It's pretty much where you go if you get kicked out or bullied at any other school, and both of those apply to me.

This place is a last resort for a lot of us, but it works well. Being here means I'm excited about my future. Everyone

has been through a lot, so I feel like I fit in. I'm not the odd one out.

At my school it was harder to feel involved in lessons because we were studying things we didn't want to be doing. Where I am now, we can select what we want to learn. The curriculum is good, and we have a lot more freedom. We're treated more like uni students, more like grown-ups, and we're very much in control of our own learning, which is great, but it takes a level of maturity.

Another thing is that the teachers really care. They tell you if you have tasks overdue, but they don't bug you about it. I would have failed by now if I'd been younger, but because of my age and because I am motivated to do well, the system works for me.

We don't have a dress code. We don't go in on Wednesdays. We can leave the class whenever we want to. It's all our responsibility. If we want to learn, then great. If we don't, we leave the room, so we don't distract the others. The teachers don't get into an argument with us about it.

Because everyone has had bad experiences, we kind of stick together. None of us have lost the ability to learn, but we don't stand for bullying.

In my last school I learnt how to study and how to get along with a lot of people, and these are important lessons. Here I have learnt more about how I best take in information, what works and what doesn't work for me.

I've worked out that I find it really easy to learn from YouTube videos, breaking down the information and using the pictures I can see, so being able to watch a video or interact with someone who knows a lot about the topic works really well.

I try to stay away from reading. My teachers will let me sit in class and watch a video. They know that's how I best digest information.

> **Top Tip from Po:** Because I want to get into design, I find that dyslexia helps me a lot. It's a perk because you need to think originally and not just recreate something someone else has already made. They want you to be able to see things from a different point of view and solve problems from a different perspective.

Spelling's still hard for me and all the English comprehension is quite hard – being able to look over information and develop an understanding of it. I get a lot of answers wrong because I misread the questions. I find that if I keep rereading the question and keep trying it usually helps. It's hard to write paragraphs with the structure we need to use in Australia, which is Topic, Explanation, Evidence, Link.

As well as dyslexia, I've also got ADHD, so I hyperfixate on different things. This helps me learn as I can now choose topics I'm passionate about. My main strategy for surviving at school would be to pick things you are going to want to know about.

Something else that's helped me is to find ways to have continuous repetition in order to learn things. Flashcards work well. I find that if I stick a sticker onto my flashcard pack that has all the topics on it, and then I stick one onto my computer, it will keep triggering my brain to think about the topic and ingrain it in my memory.

Top Tip from Po: Spelling has gotten easier as I've gotten older because people have kind of stopped caring as much, especially with arts subjects. When I was a kid, they said that people would always care, but they really don't. If they can read it, as long as it's close enough you'll be fine.

Find Enthusiastic People

Another thing that helps is to find people who are passionate about similar topics as you are to talk to, or just find people who are passionate in general. They will make you want to learn. Otherwise, your enthusiasm will decrease. Being near those with a good mindset helps a lot. We pull emotions from our peers.

My friends know I have dyslexia. There's a lot of banter, but I have stopped caring about that as I've grown up. It's just one of the things we laugh about. I can't really change being dyslexic and it's made me head in the direction of arts and that's fun. There are plenty of others at school with dyslexia or other conditions and we all get along. I stopped seeing it as a disability and started seeing it as part of me, something I have to live with. This makes it a lot easier to deal with, to be honest.

If I send someone a message, some people will nitpick about the spelling and it's annoying when they add a star and then spell the word correctly. This is the number one way to annoy me.

Having said that, I do get people to check before I post anything online just in case, though I don't do much social media.

I have quite a problem with what I call time blindness, turning up to things late. I'm also not good with making plans, as I want to do things right now. Luckily, I only live 10–15 minutes from school, so I usually get there on time. In my old school I barely turned up to the first class.

My biggest supporter has been my mum. She has talked me through a lot of things and pushed my schools to help me. She's the kind of person that if I told her I wasn't happy at school, she'd be like, 'All right. Where do you want to move to?' She'd go into school and say 'What's going on?' if I was struggling, and that really helped. I don't think I'd be here without her. I wouldn't have the same education. I would have dropped out by now. She's helped me get through a bunch of stuff.

My dad as well is the kind of person who supports me no matter what. If the school gave me a detention for doing something and I didn't do it, my dad would go to the school and tell them, 'My child didn't do this'. So over the years it's been a combination of my mum and my dad.

Dad really stands up for me. Mum pushes the school to keep me going.

Listen to Us

The most important way to help anyone with dyslexia is to listen to them. We are all different, we won't all have the same preferences about how we're treated. None of us are dumb, we just need someone to understand how we learn. This can be especially challenging for someone with dyslexia who doesn't want help because they feel they can do it all on their own. Sometimes that isn't possible.

My message to anyone at school now is just keep going. When you're at your lowest, it can only get better, and it will get better.

At my previous school I was struggling with my grades and my mental health. That was hard. I found that once I moved here, this was a fresh start. Sometimes everyone needs a change. By this time, I had learnt from my mum how to speak to the teachers and ask for what I wanted, instead of someone doing this for me or me just agreeing to things. Life gets easier when you can learn to find your voice.

I now have the whole world ahead of me. My goal is to get as high a mark as I can in my exams and figure out the future from there. A lot of people have told me that if I can get into a university course, I can always change it. I can change from automotive design to web design or graphic design. I have more confidence to take this approach; I'm not confined by what other people want me to do.

Working out what you want to do in the future can take a long time, and we all change. Just keep going, because it gets easier. I never thought I would be feeling as good and doing as well as I am now. Hell no!

> **"There are plenty of others at school with dyslexia or other conditions and we all get along. I stopped seeing it as a disability and started seeing it as part of me, something I have to live with. It makes it a lot easier to deal with, to be honest."**

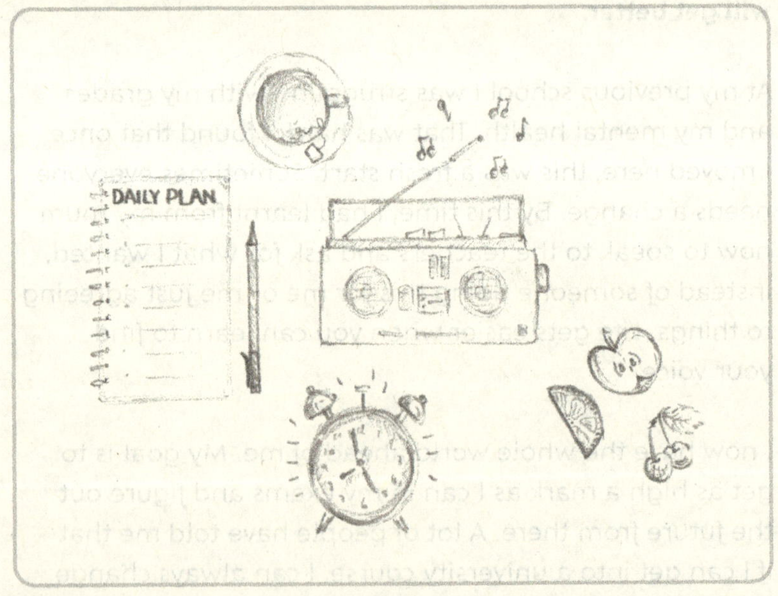

LOLA

SAM, 24, LONDON, ENGLAND

"When I'm proofreading emails or checking data, I'm very slow at it, but I'm accurate because that has been drilled into me. I check and check again. I even read a sentence backwards, as that helps me pick up on tiny mistakes. It means your mind can't fill in the gaps for you. You spot the words you've left out."

After school I went to university to study biology, and then did a master's degree in cancer biology.

Cell biology was the bit I enjoyed most. I liked all the processes and diagrams and things that were very visual. Cancer biology was particularly interesting because of the changes you can see in the affected cells.

The great thing for me was that even in exams, you're allowed to draw diagrams, so it's a different way of working. For my revision, I wouldn't write notes. I just did these huge diagrams with maybe a few words on each one, and I revised by looking at the pictures I'd drawn that showed me why something might be working the way it is.

I think university suited me more than school. When I was at school, I had the feeling of, 'Oh, they all seem to be ahead of me'. At university I might not be doing the same courses or subjects as others, but I was getting similar results. It felt good to fit in.

The way you learn at university is a lot more individual. A lot of the time you're doing independent study, so you're figuring out your own way of doing things. There are lectures, and a lot of them are recorded, so you can find your own way of learning and revising.

Working life is more regimented. My job is in medical communications and client services. I've had to work out how to work in a way that suits me.

> **Top Tip from Sam:** I've realized that I'm good at working in short bursts. I can do an hour of intense work, and then I need to go off and walk around and think about what I'm doing for a bit. Then I can go back to work half an hour later. What I can't do is concentrate solidly for an eight-hour day.

If I get a load of emails, I take a walk or have a coffee before I go into them, because it will take me a while to warm up to the task. Once I start, I take time to comprehend what the emails are asking, especially as corporate language can be so difficult. Having worked out the best way for me to work, it's all gone very well.

My dyslexia was picked up at primary school and they were good with helping me, but in secondary school there's a whole kind of different expectation with grammar and spelling. It's all about where the apostrophe goes and things like that. Hard.

I had to focus on English so much that I didn't do as well

as I should have in maths, which was what I was really good at. I thought I might fail English, so I worked on it a lot and did a lot of revision. This meant my maths mark ended up being too low so I couldn't do the subject I wanted later on, but it does mean I understand grammar rules, so it was probably a good thing.

I was relieved when I left school. I then felt nervous to go to university but soon realized it was easier than I thought it would be, and it was a good environment with friends around me.

Working Life

I've focused so much during my education on trying to work with my dyslexia, that in my working life I am careful to apply these ways.

When I'm proofreading emails or checking data, I'm very slow at it, but I'm accurate because that has been drilled into me. I have to check and check again. I even read a sentence backwards, as that helps me pick up on tiny mistakes. It means your mind can't fill in the gaps for you. You spot the words you've left out.

Top Tip from Sam: I set my system to have a two minute delay before the emails are sent out. This means you can look back at what you've written and think, 'OK, that doesn't make sense', and stop it from sending. Definitely important.

My job is to do with lung disease, so it's science based but it's also about communicating with clients. One thing I find difficult is taking minutes for calls and meetings. I have to ask at the beginning of the call 'Can this be recorded?' because I know I won't be able to keep up with the minutes. No matter how hard I try, I just can't transcribe a call. I can't remember what someone said two seconds ago, especially if it's filled with numbers or statements without context, or scientific terms, or corporate acronyms. If you can record it you can go over it and see what you've missed.

> **Top Tip from Sam:** I've told people in my team that I have dyslexia. This gives them important information about me. It means they know that if they get an email from me that doesn't quite make sense, instead of them thinking I'm not doing my job properly or I'm being lazy, they'll come back to me and ask what I meant.

There are things I've learnt to manage organizationally. I have to log my time for each project, which is quite difficult when you're distracted with other tasks to remember. I've worked around this by using spreadsheets or apps on my phone.

I'm surprised at how often my brain interprets something in a weird way that no one else's does, but knowing this can happen makes it avoidable. Sometimes I reply to someone and realize that this isn't what they've meant; I've answered the question in my head, not the one on the paper. The thing is that none of this stops me doing my job well. I just have to think a little bit differently about how I'm going to do it and come from things at a different angle.

Help When I Was Young

The support I had at the back end of primary school is the main thing that's helped me. My reading was very poor then, and I remember not wanting to read out loud in class. It's terrifying. I hope they do less of that in schools now, because some kids just can't deal with it.

My teacher Miss Waterman set up what she called the Future Authors Club. She would take five or six of us with dyslexia into a small classroom and read and write with us. She helped me never to worry about the future, and it's turned out fine.

Sometimes I still get the same feeling as the worry I had when I was reading out loud in school. We were doing some training at work, and I was asked to take minutes. Halfway through I gave up because I just couldn't track what was being said. I explained to them I was dyslexic, and they said, 'If you ask your team, they'll let you record it.' This showed me everything was fine. There's a way around problems.

Supporting someone with dyslexia, you have to get the level right. My family supported me well. There's a balance between pushing too hard, especially with reading or writing, and supporting and understanding. It can be really frustrating seeing other kids write and read. I think it's overlooked how annoying that feeling is, and how isolating.

Top Tip from Sam: It's so important to focus on someone's strengths as well. When I was younger, I was very good at maths and science, and no one ever really mentioned that, just because my reading was so poor.

The way I think dyslexia affects my friendships is that if I don't think about something after it's been said to me, it slips from my mind. So if a friend says, 'We should meet up next week', and I'm not thinking about it afterwards, I will forget that they've ever said that. I need it to be repeated to me or someone to follow up and say, 'Were we going to meet?' I've got the calendars and apps on my phone with constant reminders about everything. I get reminded three days before, a day before... I need that repetition, so it sticks in my head.

Because I have this system in place, the good thing is that I remember anniversaries and birthdays and things like that. I wonder if having dyslexia can make you quite thoughtful because you know you're forgetful most of the time so you make an effort not to forget.

I use social media, but I don't post. I lurk in the background and comment and like. I worry about my spelling even in texts and comments. I make sure everything is spelt perfectly because that's been so engrained in me, even though it doesn't matter. I correct every mistake.

Reading aloud at school dents your confidence. It makes you think when you're older that you can't do things like public speaking or job interviews or presentations, but I'm actually good at them. Just because you can't do one thing doesn't mean you can't do something else.

I think anyone reading this could look for jobs where dyslexia won't be much of a problem, but I've always had the mindset that I'm going to apply for whatever jobs and not consider dyslexia as a factor. Once you're in it, there are always ways of working around things. There are so many tools online like AI and stuff to check your work and help you proofread.

It can be daunting seeing a job description and thinking, 'I'm not going to be good at writing emails or reading other people's work', but there are so many ways to help yourself. We need a mindset of 'Right, I can do this'. You're going to get frustrated, and a corporate environment is all about deadlines, so you've just got to be ready. When they say, 'Can I have this back in half an hour?', you need to calm yourself down and remind yourself how capable you are.

The office environment is challenging. There's a bit less space for creativity. There's less space for visual learning. But I don't go into work thinking, 'I'm dyslexic, I have to do this. I have to do that'. That goes away when you're in the world of work and you know what you're good at. We're all good at a lot of things, but we won't find this out unless we try. That's my best advice.

> “Sometimes I still get the same feeling as the worry I had when I was reading out loud in school. We were doing some training at work, and I was asked to take minutes. Halfway through I gave up because I just couldn’t track what was being said. I explained to them I was dyslexic, and they said, ‘If you ask your team, they’ll let you record it’. This showed me everything was fine. There’s a way around problems.”

GABRIELLA, 24, EAST LOTHIAN, SCOTLAND

"I have a job I really love, working in a drug development lab. We spin and separate drug samples and put them into a freezer where another laboratory will analyse them. There are people out there who need medication daily. What I do helps make sure that their medication is safe for them. I like knowing that I make a difference."

Most of the learning I've done in my life was during my school years, but not in my lessons. I learnt a lot outside of school – when I was with my friends, doing my homework, using the internet – finding ways that worked for me to take in information.

I used to get easily distracted because I would be looking something up and then I'd disappear down a rabbit hole of other information. I'd think, 'How did I even get here?' Then I'd have to stop myself and go back to whatever I was doing to begin with. Now that I'm an adult, I'm still learning stuff in my day to day, but not by sitting in a classroom.

I was relieved when I left school. I had some good teachers, but I never felt I really fitted in, because of dyslexia. This meant it didn't feel right being there and it was good to get away, but I missed my friends after we left, because we all went in different directions.

Some things about school still help me now. The social

aspect helped, and subjects I was quite good at like science help. When they made us speak in front of the class that was good for my confidence. I learnt in English about how to write formal letters and emails, and that helps me so much in my day-to-day life now.

But I think there was a lot more they could have taught us, especially someone like me. If I'd been taught how to do time management better that would have been great. I would have liked it if they had taught us how to understand our finances in mathematics. If they taught basic things like even how often you need to clean things, that would have been great to know before becoming an adult. I wouldn't have needed to keep running to my mum and asking her.

After school it was like 'OK, you must apply for jobs and courses. You must find a way to make money. You must move out. You must be an adult and remember to do all the adult things like finance and housework'. That's what I was faced with, and I felt a little lost.

I decided to do a foundation degree science course. This meant two years studying instead of three because I wasn't confident enough to do a dissertation.

In secondary school, it had been all exams, but at university I was mainly graded on coursework or assignments, and I had to reference everything I did. I had to figure out how to do this and I wasn't great at it. For some reason I was better at exams. I always think with exams you know more or less what the questions will be, and if you've done the prep beforehand, you can study the material in a way that clicks into your brain. Assignments were all due in the same two weeks and I found that hard.

My foundation degree limited my options, but it has led to a job I really love. I work in a drug development lab. We spin and separate drug samples and put them into a freezer where another laboratory will analyse them. We do a lot of printing labels, labelling tubes, and a lot of paperwork. There are people out there who need medication daily. What I do helps make sure that their medication is safe for them. I like knowing that I make a difference.

Because I adore science, especially biology, I like learning how the different elements of what we're doing interact with each other. I like that if I ask a question, a lot of people will give a response, and I learn something. I am constantly learning every day.

We do a lot of prioritizing, so it has taken me a while to get to where I am now, where I know what's more important.

I have good attention to detail when it's not my own work, so I'm not entirely sure how that works. My brain doesn't seem to recognize my work as something it needs to rewrite, read, or do something else to, because it knows it's what I wrote. But when it comes to other people's work, it's as if my brain just switches to, 'That should be this. This should be that.'

Because of my dyslexia, I have a bad habit of misreading

things. It happens fairly often that my brain will switch a word round or switch a letter round, and for the most part, there's normally no damage done, but it can be infuriating where I've just checked something or written something and I then had to relook at it and spend more time doing it because my brain's just gone, 'Oops, I'm switching that'.

I have to find coping mechanisms that allow me to work efficiently. For example, sometimes when I'm working, I have music playing, especially if I'm doing a routine task, because it helps me stay focused and drowns out other thoughts. Other times, I need to be talking to someone just to get my thoughts out there, otherwise my brain tends to run off rambling to itself, and I make more mistakes.

> **Top Tip from Gabriella:** I find making a priority list of what I need to get done means I remember more and gives me structure. Having structure is the biggest thing that helps.

I also have Autocorrect on everything. My laptop has Autocorrect, my phone has Autocorrect. If they didn't, I would be afraid of publishing anything where anyone could read it.

I think, if anything, dyslexia helps me with my friendships, because by pure coincidence a lot of my friends are neurodivergent in some way. There's something about being neurodivergent that means you just click with other neurodivergent people better than you would with someone who's maybe not so much.

All through my life my mum has been a rock. She started off not knowing much about dyslexia. When we found out, she talked me through it. Even when I probably didn't want it, she would be pushing me to take the help she knew I needed. She fought with my education department so much that I'm pretty sure they avoided her calls.

Like my mum, anyone who cares for someone with dyslexia needs to be very patient. You need to ask not what they need, but what they think they need. Let them talk it out. Sometimes they won't be able to explain it. It's worth suggesting if they'd like to try one method. If that method doesn't work, suggest others. There are loads of different ways to help, and to let them help themselves.

As a child it's harder to talk to an adult or authority figure, so you have to fight the battle for them. As they get more experienced, support them in standing up for themselves.

Top Tip from Gabriella: I suggest looking for courses that could help, such as cooking, time management, or planning skills – something that supports them in their daily tasks. If you're dyslexic, you can be more forgetful and you can fail to keep every task you need to do in your head. With me when I start the first task, I forget what the other four I need to do are, unless they're written down.

When you're at school you have people you know and your family and friends around you. You have a bit more of a support group. After school you have a new life, a new environment, and you have to start from scratch to find a new structure and make sure all your responsibilities are on your to-do list.

The more we can organize ourselves and understand ourselves, the more we can achieve. I want to travel and see the world. I want to see how things are outside of the world that I've already lived in. What I've experienced is such a small part of what there is out there. There's so much more waiting for me in my future.

"When you're at school you have people you know and your family and friends around you. You have a bit more of a support group. After school you have a new life, a new environment, and you have to start from scratch to find a new structure and make sure all your responsibilities are on your to-do list."

RACHEL, 19, OXFORD, ENGLAND

"When I'm studying now, I know I won't remember anything unless I understand it. This made me realize I have to ask questions. If I was ever worried at school about asking a question in front of the class, I would wait behind and ask the teacher at the end of the lesson. That's how important understanding is for me."

Dyslexia has never felt like a bad thing for me. Knowing I had it was good. It was the reason why I found some things hard. It's just something different about you, but only in the same way that people are different from each other anyway.

Learning Through Mistakes

I learnt how it's best for me to revise quite early on, when I was doing my GCSEs.* I realized that I learn best through making mistakes. I don't know if it's because I'm a perfectionist, but I blurt everything about a topic down on my whiteboard and then I go over it with a red pen and rub out the bits I got wrong and write them correctly. Then I find I don't forget them because I don't want to make the mistake again.

I'm at university doing biomedical science and I still use that method now.

* GCSEs are exams taken in most of the UK at 16

When I'm studying now, I picture something I'm trying to make sense of, but I know I won't remember anything unless I understand it. This made me realize I have to ask questions. If I was ever worried at school about asking a question in front of the class, I would wait behind and ask the teacher at the end of the lesson. That's how important understanding is for me.

The other thing that helps me is linking things. If I link something I've learnt to something else I've learnt, then I remember it better. I get satisfaction from seeing those links.

I'm quite anti essays. For me, they are a combination of not knowing how to express my thoughts, while also wanting my work to be really good because I'm a perfectionist.

This combination means that I really can't write something down if I don't think it's good. I just sit there with a blank page. I've never understood why I can answer something out loud, but I can't write it down.

This is less of a thing with science essays, as they're quite different. You're just making points in a logical way to make it clear to the reader. You're not using an interesting structure that requires consideration of multiple criteria at once, which you have to in English. A whole extra layer.

Also we write so many essays at university, you learn not to expect the high standard with everything.

Typing Helps

One thing that has really helped is my tutor at university suggesting I could type essays. I was reluctant because I'm not the quickest typer, but I find it puts less pressure on me. You can edit what you write on a computer if you don't like it.

Handwriting feels permanent and you have to cross it out if you don't want it there. When I did this I worried that my work would look messy and would be harder to follow, and this could affect my grade. I wouldn't have wanted to type at school though because no one else was, but at university, everyone uses their laptop.

At my university there are essays all the time. I knew this would happen, but I didn't want to be studying somewhere where there would only be a few and thoughts about the essays would build up inside me. I would rather get used to the essays, and then they won't seem such a big deal.

I've always been confused by the stereotype that people with dyslexia are less clever than people without it. I think dyslexia just means you might need a different method for learning the things that you struggle with. This isn't always provided in schools, and it took me a while to work out the methods that helped me.

I found it too hard to think of ideas and write them down because I knew people would be reading and judging them. Luckily for me my mum understood the problem and knew I wasn't just being lazy. There was something blocking me. It was hard when everyone else was writing something in class and I was there with a blank page.

Top Tip from Rachel: When I was really struggling with writing essays at school, sometimes my mum told me to say things out loud to get me started, and once I'd started it was much easier to carry on. I often expressed thoughts better out loud than when I had to write them down. I found the blank page very intimidating.

Even now, after years of not doing English, when I sit down to work, I think, 'Well, at least it's not an English essay'. That's how I make myself feel better. I am so grateful I'm not doing English.

If you're struggling at school now, I know it's hard at the moment, but it will be over at some point. It's not a life-long thing, and there are loads of things you can do after school. Then you'll be able to think, 'At least I'm not doing English anymore'.

"I've always been confused by the stereotype that people with dyslexia are less clever than people without it. I think dyslexia just means you might need a different method for learning the things that you struggle with. This isn't always provided in schools, and it took me a while to work out the methods that helped me."

MALEAH, 19, MANCHESTER, ENGLAND

“I’ve had a lot of part-time jobs, including lifeguarding and swim teaching, which I’m still doing. Dyslexia has helped me to understand that not all kids learn the same. It’s taught me to adapt to different children.”

After school I went to university to study mental health nursing. It’s challenging, but also fun and interesting. I’m doing two placements this year, one on a men’s ward and one on a geriatric ward.

Originally, I wanted to do educational psychology. I didn’t get the grades, but I’m not disappointed. I think mental health nursing suits me better because it’s more practical. Children’s mental health intrigues me the most, but I’m not sure yet what I’m going to specialize in.

When I was younger, I worried I wouldn’t get into university. I was fine at school until about Year 4 when I was 8 or 9 when they noticed there was a bit of a gap between how I was doing in English and what they expected. I was very behind. I was diagnosed in Year 5, and then they gave me extra English lessons when the class was doing different subjects.

I had extra time in my SATs* and more support in

* SATs in the UK are usually taken at 10–11, and measure performance in English and Maths

secondary school, so instead of doing a second language I did extra English again. I ended up getting an A in English literature and I passed English language, so that extra help was important.

Top Tip from Maleah: I remember in history I was looking for different strategies to help me and I found one that stuck. I had to write out what I was trying to learn, then read it out loud to myself. That would help me to see the mistakes I'd made and improve my writing.

I also went to the Waltham Forest Dyslexia Association with lots of other people my age. That helped show me I wasn't alone and improved my English at the same time. I am motivated to accept help. I've always been someone who wants to do well.

I've had a lot of part-time jobs. I started working as a hairdressing assistant when I was about 15. Then I worked at a local leisure centre as a receptionist, and I moved on to lifeguarding and swim teaching, which I'm still doing. Dyslexia has helped me in swim teaching to understand that not all kids learn the same. It's taught me to adapt to different children.

My memory and communication skills aren't always the best when I'm teaching and this can hold me back, but most of the time it's been good. Sometimes when I'm trying to communicate stuff from my head and speak it out, it gets a bit lost. I deal with this by setting out my plan for the lesson before it starts. I always take my time and don't rush anything.

When I left school, I was quite excited to be honest. It felt like a chance to explore different things, live by myself, and become more independent.

Some of what I learnt in my school years helps me now. History has helped me communicate with patients, not just when I'm dealing with older people. I had one young person with autism on the mental health ward and he liked to give me facts every day, so I gave him some facts back. A lot of the other things I learnt at school don't feel that relevant to be honest.

I think I learn best when I do this thing called the blurting technique. I read some information, talk about what I've read to other people, and then write it out. They told me about it at school, but I also saw someone doing it on TikTok.

My long-term memory is a lot better than my short-term memory, so this can help me. Also, because I'm a visual person, once I can see something it normally sticks in my brain. If I see a patient with a particular condition, I remember the details. Taking my time and taking breaks is great for me, as well as visualizing my goals and why I want to achieve them.

Because I've had dyslexia for the whole of my life, I don't really know what it's like not having it. My family is half-Jamaican and half-British, and they have always been supportive. When I was younger, my parents kept trying to find different ways to help me and get me support. I use technology to help me as well, speaking into a voice machine for Instagram and TikTok so the spelling's OK.

I think what's most important for anyone struggling at school is for teachers to meet with their parents and understand how learning is different for each one, and what they all struggle with so they can help. They need to make time for that.

Give Yourself Time

The other important thing is for us to accept help when it's offered. Dealing with dyslexia is not the easiest thing to do, but you will get there. It just takes time.

At university I get extensions on all my assessments and exams. I also get other support – I was given a one-on-one tutor and more funding. They gave me a printer because I like to print out copies, not just see writing on a screen.

At the end of the year, I have to give the printer back to the unit and then apply for another one next year.

Being with my friends at school was fun, but after school you have the freedom to do what you want and be more in control of your life. I like that. When I'm older I'd like to work abroad, maybe in Toronto. I've researched different places where they speak English and that's the one I've come up with.

I still get my words muddled up, but I think that's my only struggle to be honest. Anything with spelling I use technology, and life does get easier.

If you're still at school now, try not to stress about it. You will get there; it's just going to take a little bit more time. If you put in the effort, you will see the benefits.

> "Being with my friends at school was fun, but after school you have the freedom to do what you want and be more in control of your life."

CHAPTER 5

Never Look Back

JOE, 19, WEST LOTHIAN, SCOTLAND

"My college course was disappointing, there was too much sitting around in classrooms. So I left and threw myself in at the deep end by starting a bushcraft adventure business. I am teaching children about the outdoors, which is a big passion of mine."

On my last day, I walked out of the school door and realized how much more there is to the world than what my exam results would say.

Straightaway I started running my own business, teaching lessons for children and young people. I was big into BMX at the skate park, so I started teaching BMX classes and I also taught road safety for cyclists.

I decided I would enrol in a college course in outdoor adventure, and another course in leadership pursuit. After a short while, I was disappointed with these. I was expecting the courses to be a little bit more hands-on, but there was too much sitting around in classrooms. It felt like I was going to waste time waiting around getting qualifications and I asked myself if I needed to do this.

Instead, I left. I threw myself in at the deep end and started a bushcraft adventure business, teaching children about the outdoors, which is a big passion of mine. I'm seriously into nature and how it's so important that people reconnect with the natural world right now.

I immediately saw how much better my life was. I ran my own schedule, and I wasn't just following what other people thought I should do. I was doing what I loved, and other people loved it too.

All of these experiences and the decision to follow my instincts taught me valuable lessons. They gave me the confidence to set up what I'm doing now. I'm in the process of starting a whole new education system. It's in the woods just along the road from where I live, and together with my mum and my auntie I'm going to be taking on all the kids who are told they're not going to fit in at a normal school and that they'll never amount to anything.

We're trying to re-channel all of their energy and use it for something more positive, showing them the benefits of being outdoorsy and learning everything there is to learn in the wild that nature can teach us.

Especially for children and young people with dyslexia, I think being stuck in a sweat box of a classroom, behind a desk all day, is not the way to be successful.

As we've been developing this, we've been learning as we go along. It's not all easy. The marketing side is always my downfall, but I have to work my way around it and get better at it. I've got to just do my best.

The content of the lessons is something I've always been interested in since I was a young kid, but it's not something I managed to be involved with as much as I wanted. My friends preferred playing on Xbox and that kind of thing, so I usually joined them with that. As I got older I managed to separate myself and realize that the outdoors is where I wanted to spend my time, going into the woods, doing my own research, and learning about different plants, trees, and mushrooms.

No one should be forced into something that makes them feel uncomfortable, and I realized I'm not very good at learning from someone else. I'm good at educating myself. If there's something that I'm passionate about, it makes it so much easier for me to pick it up.

Looking back to school, in my head it just feels like a big waste of time. With my work now I'm spending so much time with children who are homeschooled, and I see how much they're able to develop their own individual personalities from a young age. I can see how well they develop the skills that they'll want to be good at when they're older.

It's crazy how many people I know who are my age still have no idea who they are as a person, because they've been made to sit down and told what to do their whole life. These kids who have been able to learn at their own pace know so much more about what they want their futures to look like.

Primary school was difficult for me. With high school I got on much better with my teachers. I did all the practical subjects I was strong in, and I was top of the class in them, which was great for me as I was totally able to embrace who I was as a person. This meant that if I was ever picked on, it wasn't something that I let get to me because I was so sure of who I was. Anyone trying to give me a hard time just felt irrelevant.

Maybe I'd had enough of education because I got to the point in my college course where my enthusiasm naturally dwindled away. I had a feel for what they were trying to teach, and it was enough of a taster to allow me to strive to do the things I'm doing now. I'm working with more challenging groups of children who were getting chucked out of the classroom all the time. These are kids who struggled so much in school but are absolutely the best people you could ever take outside to do an activity. They couldn't be more enthusiastic about just being outside. It sounds so simple, but it makes all the difference to them.

I remember when I was at school the days like these were the ones that become those you remember forever. Why wouldn't you want to have those days every day?

When I think back to school I think there's not much that I learnt there that helps me now, certainly nothing my parents couldn't have taught me themselves, like learning to count or telling the time or reading simple things. There's nothing I learnt in high school that I use every day.

Learning Drama May Have Helped Me

Having said that, one of my courses at school was in drama, and to do that you have to be quite charismatic and have confidence, so that may be useful when I'm talking to a group of kids. But I was always a confident person – because of my dyslexia I had to be confident, or just sit down and shut up and say nothing.

Another of my exams was in woodwork, and that inspired me to go out and do more on my own. At home I started making walking sticks, and I have a home forge, so I made axes and jewellery. Unfortunately at school these departments had very little funding, but the teachers did their best.

> **Top Tip from Joe:** The good things that come with dyslexia help me all the time. I think it's the way my brain processes information. If I'm out in the woods and trying to remember different plant species that I've just noticed, I have a technique to make sure the new names go into my brain. I think of rhyming words to help me.

Dyslexia has helped me with problem solving too. At school I was always having to do something in a different way from everyone else. This gave me the confidence to try things that somebody else wouldn't have thought of. Like if I'm in the woods, building a shelter, I think of all possibilities: 'What's going to happen if a big wind catches it in this direction?', that kind of thing. I have to think a little bit deeper and go that little bit further to get the answers.

Fun Is Important

I use storytelling skills too. One of the things I learnt in my college course was that if you're teaching kids anything, the most important thing is to make sure they're having fun. If you're able to get them excited about what you're talking about, kids are going to pick it up so much quicker. If you're just shouting at them and pointing at a blackboard, they're going to be uninterested. You have to be excited with them.

If they're not interested in what they're doing and they want to go off and build something in a sandpit, they need to do what they need to do. Maybe in 20 minutes they'll feel calmer and will come back and listen.

The only things that make my working life difficult are the writing and reading. I struggled with these so much at school and I just threw myself into the subjects that interested me more. You need to look at the positives and realize what you are good at. If there's a lot of reading and writing to do for the business, it gets delegated to my mum or my auntie, while I dig the big holes for the fire pits.

I learnt about delegation at school because when we were working in groups, I was never the person who was asked to write the script or read it out for everyone, but they knew I was the one who could give the presentation off the top of my head. Everyone has their place in a team.

Life has taught me to follow what's most important to you. Always. Because that's going to be the thing you're going to succeed in, no matter how impossible this might sound to someone else, or if you're called weird for wanting to do it. Just do the thing that's going to make you happy, stay with it, and stay driven to achieve your goal. You could have all the money in the world and be in a job that you absolutely hate and be depressed your whole life. Then when you look back when you're old, how would you feel about how you spent all those years?

> **Top Tip from Joe:** Whatever you decide to do, there's always going to be a bump in the road. Something will go wrong. It's how you deal with those problems and how you stay positive about them that matters. If you let things feel like they're beating you up, you start letting yourself believe that you can't do something. All of a sudden, you're going to find a lot more things you can't do.

I think life with dyslexia has become easier for me. In primary it felt like such a big deal, and it got in the way of making friends with people, but when you grow up and get in the real world you realize it matters so much less. It gives you strengths other people don't have. Writing texts is a problem – they end up taking me 20 minutes, typing and retyping the things. Social media isn't great. It's one of those things I've always struggled with, keeping up to date with posting things for work and stuff like that. I am quite good at scheduling meetings, but it has to be done my way for me to remember. It's not a control freak thing, the information just doesn't stick in my head. I would always rather have something written on a piece of paper than have everything on digital.

Over the years my mum and dad have had my back through every single part of my dyslexia journey. They have always encouraged me to do what makes me happy. They never said, 'No, you need to go and do this job. You need to stay in school.' They just trusted me.

The most important thing anyone supporting someone with dyslexia can do is to be patient. Try to trust them. They will have their way of doing things that works for them. Don't try to force your way on them, because to deal with dyslexia they really do have superpowers. To learn to use these properly is the best thing.

On my last day of school, I felt instant relief. It was just that feeling of freedom, of being out of that education system. High school can cause so much mental discomfort for people with all the stress at a time when your body's already going through enough changes. I see with the kids I work with now the difference that it makes being away from that school load.

Classrooms Never Change

The school system right now is broken. It's not possible to get it right for every child. Teachers are underfunded and overstressed. Trying to get kids to learn the way that works for them is important. Cars have changed over the years, houses have changed, classrooms still have someone standing in front and everyone else sat at a desk. There's been no ingenuity or forward thinking.

That setup doesn't work for everyone. If it doesn't work for you, it's not your fault. Be true to yourself and things will start to fall into place. Life can become so much better.

> **"Life has taught me to follow what's most important to you. Always. Because that's going to be the thing you're going to succeed in, no matter how impossible this might sound to someone else, or if you're called weird for wanting to do it. Just do the thing that's going to make you happy, stay with it, and stay driven to achieve your goal."**

ADDISON, 18, OHIO, USA

> "At work the positive things about dyslexia help you, especially if you do a lot of hands-on stuff like I do. The big thing about dyslexia is that our brains work in a different way. Working in 3D almost comes naturally to me."

Ever since I was a boy, I've loved cars. I'm now studying High Performance Automotive, building race car engines at the University of Northwestern Ohio.

I think if you have dyslexia, you don't have to go to college. I did it because I was set on what I wanted to do. College isn't worth it if it's something that you don't want to do, or something you don't obsess over.

Sophomore year* I was working out what I wanted to go into, and I made it into my high school's auto tech programme. My high school was unusual because they offered 13 different programmes and auto tech was one of them. Schools like mine are called career tech schools and you either do your classes online while learning a trade or go through the school.

Work Release

I was lucky because my auto tech teacher was into drag

* 10th grade of high school in the USA, for ages 15–16

racing and that opened me up to high performance. When I was in senior year,* I found I could do my other classes online, and the rest of the time do work release.

So I got a job at Ford working 40 or 50 hour weeks, getting school done in the rest of the time. For a year I was a mobile mechanic, working on US Postal Service mail trucks, doing the maintenance and going on the road whenever they had a breakdown, replacing whatever had gone wrong.

Working in 3D almost comes naturally to me. At least in this kind of stuff I feel ahead. My brain works in a logical way, too. It's like 'That goes here, that goes there'. There's a lot of the job that's just you knowing how it all goes back together.

When I graduated, I finished that job. Now I'm at Northwestern Ohio from Monday to Thursday, and working at Ford on Fridays, weekends, and holiday breaks.

I found it easy doing my schoolwork online. There was always a teacher I could contact and ask what was going on if I didn't understand. Sometimes I had to go in for two or three hours to see them. Because of dyslexia, schoolwork took me longer than other people, but I'm just used to sucking that up now.

When I left high school, I was kind of happy, relieved to be out of the system. I guess the American public system

* Senior year is 12th grade of high school, for ages 17–18

isn't very good for kids with disabilities. It's hard to find anyone who wants to be a teacher and specialize in that.

At work the positive things about dyslexia help you, especially if you do a lot of hands-on stuff like I do. The big thing about dyslexia is that our brains work in a different way. We know how to put things back together.

Pushing Myself to Read

At the college I am at now, there is a bit of reading and mine is better than it was. I've really pushed myself, ever since I started there. My handwriting has gotten so much better. In so many classes you don't have to use the computer, and I really like to write my notes down for some reason. I'm trying harder in some of these basics than I did at public school. Maybe I feel more motivated now to do well.

Doing what I do, you really need to know what goes into a car. You have to do your homework, and if you do, your effort pays off. You can probably get the hands-on stuff done quicker than anyone else, and in this field there are not enough people who can do these things fast. There are people who know how everything works and how everything moves but not enough to do things quickly. It takes a while to learn this.

There are a lot of kids here who haven't been working in the field. I was already a mechanic when I started here and now I'm here to be a better mechanic and a better technician. Work experience couldn't be more useful.

I feel like in the last year and a half I've learnt more than I have throughout high school. I think all the way up from kindergarten until sixth grade,* that's the stuff you really need to know, that's like the basics. It's what you need to be part of society. Besides that, I think I started learning a lot in the automotive programme at school. I was lucky to have a teacher who was part of this industry.

Top Tip from Addison: When you hear guys talking about what you want to know, you just sit there and soak it up like a sponge, picking up all the information you need.

If anyone is interested in going into the field I'm in, I'd say you have to develop a thick skin. People say stuff to you that sounds mean or unsettling, but they mean it in a good way. It may sound harsh, but if you're working on a vehicle that's worth thousands and thousands of dollars, it makes sense that you have to be pushed to do a good job. That's why you have to do your homework. You can't just think, 'This will work'.

I think everything's been harder for me than it was for kids who didn't struggle with reading. I have ADHD as well, and that's another thing. I hyperfocus on something and then I realize I've missed 30 minutes of a lecture. Even if I get behind, I have to keep on going. My ADHD means I'll think about something else, even though I'm still reading. Then I realize I'm not really taking anything in. Or I get lost in the spaces between words. Reading is the hardest thing.

* Roughly 5–12 (kindergarten until sixth grade)

Finishing high school was good, and it's going to feel good once I'm out of college too. I'm looking ahead and I have a lot of goals. You can't do anything without goals. I just want to get out there and master my craft.

I think the programme I'm on is probably the best you can do. There are so many people in the industry who've gone through this programme and are running or working on stuff like Formula One. GT3 is also pretty big.

Since I'm at Ford, I really like the Coyote engine. I enjoy working on the platform that's coming with the Mustangs and the F150s. Eventually I want to work in the world of drag racing or street racing.

In school, they shoved a bunch of electrical classes on me and that helps me understand how the computer in a car relates to everything's that's going on. Computers are a big deal for understanding how a modern car works, and how different sensors communicate with each other. When a car is upgraded you have to know this, to tune the vehicle to operate correctly with its new high-performance parts. When I was 15, I built my own PC, and I've been interested in computers ever since.

Finding a Mentor

I've been networking, which is so important in this industry, and I'm talking to this tuning guy and he's said he will mentor me, which is great because tuning is what I'm planning on doing after I finish here. I want to leave an impact on the automotive community.

I think it'd be cool to master something and be the best at something.

I have come a long way. A lot of people can be ignorant about dyslexia, but I don't let this affect me. I've worked hard enough in this field and know enough and have studied enough. When you actually meet someone in the same field, and you're into the same things, it's like, 'Wow, dyslexia really doesn't matter'.

My girlfriend has been supportive. She could have been ignorant and like everyone else call me stupid, but she never did. My mom almost made it embarrassing how much she supported me, talking to other parents with kids with dyslexia. I found it annoying when I was young but appreciate it in the long run. With dyslexia, you just have to go through it. There are a lot of kids with dyslexia who don't have a good homelife and I can imagine that makes school almost impossible.

Top Tip from Addison: To anyone struggling I would say just keep going through it. There's a lot to help you now. There are programs on your computer that mark the start of every sentence in bold. I think things like that can probably help a lot, especially if you're trying to read about something you don't particularly like, or care about.

Most important is to build on friendships and make acquaintances and find people to help you. Look for people with a mutual friend on Facebook or Instagram. I found someone I worked with at Ford, texted them, and through them made contact with someone to help me. It's knowing people. It's not just luck. You have to put yourself into places that some might find uncomfortable, but if you find good people, they can help.

Life is much better now. At school you're pushed in with everyone, which is good because it helps you co-exist. In a specialized college, you're around a lot of people who like the same things as you. That helps me to be inspired. I'm working hard. Constantly doing something, constantly working. I'm aiming to be pretty successful. My goal is to get there.

> **"A lot of people can be ignorant about dyslexia, but I don't let this affect me. I've worked hard enough and know enough and have studied enough. When you actually meet someone in the same field, and you're into the same things, it's like, 'Wow, dyslexia really doesn't matter'."**

EDDIE, 21, LEEDS, ENGLAND

> **"When I was young, I struggled so much that I just thought it was all over and I'd be stuck in a low paying job. I didn't have any confidence whatsoever. I would never have thought I would be this ambitious or imagine myself with a successful business."**

My school exams went better than I expected. I thought I'd get Cs and stuff, but I ended up with a couple of As, and that allowed me to do literally whatever I wanted.

I decided to go to university, but I didn't want to go into something too academic. I also thought I might get bored quite quickly, so I wanted to do something that would involve interacting with people a lot. I went for Real Estate and Property Management. This means I'll end up being a Chartered Surveyor and I'll be setting up a business buying and doing up homes.

My plan is to buy my own properties, which I can rent and lease, and I also want to run a property turnover business where you buy homes cheap, invest money into them, and sell them on. I'm quite entrepreneurial, but I know this won't all be possible unless I have a bit of money behind me, so first I need to get a job to get my finances in place.

When I was at primary school in the early years, I would never have thought I would be this ambitious or imagine myself with a successful business. I struggled so much that I just thought it was all over and I'd be stuck in a low paying job. I didn't have any confidence whatsoever.

Everything Changed

Before they knew I was dyslexic, my teachers were always telling me to hurry up. They never gave me a break. I remember there was one piece of homework, and I just couldn't get it right. I was asked to redo it, redo it, and redo it, about six times. Eventually, my parents said this isn't right. Then a teacher suggested I get assessed for dyslexia, and by Year 6 I started getting help. All at once, everything changed, and things began to make a bit more sense. The teachers were putting things in place to help me achieve more.

After this my confidence grew and grew and grew and grew and grew. I understood why I had been struggling.

> **Top Tip from Eddie:** The best advice I could give anyone is to get the assessment done. Once that's in place you can try your best to get the building blocks anyone needs.

At the start of secondary school, in Year 7,* I was bottom set for everything, but I started to think, 'You know what, I can actually do alright here'. The teachers were just amazing. It was the book *Toe by Toe*** that set the

* Ages 11–12 in the UK

** A highly structured phonics-based teaching manual

foundation for me. I can't express how amazing *Toe by Toe* was. Without that I'd have struggled a lot. That book is the key that opened everything up for me. It allowed me to catch up with everyone else. My reading age went from eight years old when I was 11 to pretty much the maximum score in reading tests within a year and a half. It was a turnaround. By the end of Year 8 or beginning of Year 9 I was pretty much top set for everything.

My Teacher Gave Me Confidence

One of my teachers in secondary school was Mrs Platt. She gave me two or three one-on-one lessons a week. Honestly, I can't thank her enough. She was so influential in giving me confidence. She didn't care how well you did. She just cared that you were making that little bit of progress. My mum, when she was young, had a properly tough, horrible time. She really struggled in school, while her twin sister went to grammar school. She's so glad I got the help.

In college, I had weekly sessions I could go to for support, but they weren't mandatory as at that stage I was on track with my learning. It's the same in university now. I've got the sessions there if I want them and I can always go and talk to people. These days I don't need to let anyone know I have dyslexia, other than the university. I just get on with things.

I think the way my education began set the foundation of ambition for me. I wanted to prove everyone wrong. In primary school I was struggling. My mum went in for a parents' evening and one of the teachers said to her, 'I can't make your son smart'. That motivated me to rub how wrong they were in their face. I remember once I saw them at an event. I know they didn't recognize me, but I didn't care. I went up to them and said, 'I am smart now, thank you'. I had to tell them that.

When I left school, I was quite happy. I felt like I had everything pretty much sorted. I needed a break from education, so I took a gap year and worked the whole time because I didn't want to take on too many loans.

Because of all the struggles with dyslexia I've always had to plan like this, to make sure I did things right.

I started off at a restaurant as a waiter while I was still at school. Then I was a kitchen porter and then I was doing food prep after school, and when I went to college they asked me if I wanted to work there full-time as a chef. They trained me up from scratch.

Top Tip from Eddie: I thought being a chef was quite fun because it was practical. I made sure I didn't struggle with my memory. I always did just three checks at a time, so I was never overwhelmed by what all the tables wanted. Everyone else might have done a million, but I managed to keep up.

Looking back now, one way that school helped me was all the social interaction. In property there's a lot of linking up with people to work on different properties, so this is a good skill to have.

One thing that's not good about school is that you always feel pushed to get As, Bs, and Cs. Unless you want to go into super academic subjects, you don't need that. For most subjects you only need simple maths and simple English to get you through. The same is true for most jobs.

Another thing is that you have all these maths formulas, all the science, and it's good to have this knowledge, but it would be better to cover how these are applied in real life. This would help set us up right for when we leave.

One of my dyslexic traits is problem solving. This comes in useful virtually every single day. When I talk to people about what I've done they go, 'Hang on, you can't have done it that way'. You picture things differently. I have always known how to break problems down into small pieces and I know that the small pieces come together into a big piece that makes sense.

I've done lots of my learning through informative YouTube videos. I find it easy to take in information in that way. I find channels that cover engineering issues, and structures and how they're built. I always thought that was better for me than school, because I'm taking the information into my mind by looking at it, instead of reading it.

Even when I'm doing my course, instead of doing a lot of reading I prefer to find videos. I have to do some reading or I'd fall behind, but the videos help me make sense of everything.

I've never been good at spelling, but having Spellcheck is more than enough. If even Spellcheck can't get what you're trying to write, you can speak to your phone now. And you can always ask what a word's definition is to double check. That's really helpful.

As you move into the world of work, I'd say confidence is everything. I don't mean that we should be big-headed. I mean have the confidence to look after yourself, get on with your work, and find your independence. I gradually developed the confidence to see the kids who were really smart and try to compete with them. I put in the work to do well.

> **"In school I was struggling. My mum went in for a parents' evening and one of the teachers said to her, 'I can't make your son smart'. That motivated me to rub how wrong they were in their face. It set the foundation of ambition in me. I remember once I saw them at an event. I know they didn't recognize me, but I didn't care. I went up to them and said, 'I am smart now, thank you'. I had to tell them that."**

LOLA

JENNY, 26, LAGOS, NIGERIA

"Even though I struggled to learn in school, I learn so much in my day-to-day life now. I think this is because my work is a lot more practical. It involves more than just having to sit down and listen to somebody talk and take notes. I am doing what I've been taught, and this helps me remember."

School caused me lots of sadness, anxiety, and panic attacks. I didn't know what these feelings were then, but now I recognize them, and I know I'm on the path to feeling better.

Imagine you're in a class and your teacher is speaking Chinese and writing Chinese on the board. Every other person in the class understands but you, being an English-speaking person, cannot. Imagine being there, going back there five days a week.

At school they were teaching in my language, and I was supposed to understand what was being said, but there was nothing I could take in. Nothing made sense to me. That was the worst thing. When I try to think back, everything about my time there seems blurry.

Despite this, one of the teachers said some of us could get to university without needing to repeat a class. He said I could go because of my behaviour and attitude, not because of my grades. I was punctual and quiet, so I was pretty much the student that every teacher wanted, even though I wasn't smart enough.

So I was given a place, and I did find uni was a lot better. I think this was partly because I was studying something I was interested in: mass communications. For the first time I started getting high marks.

I didn't receive any extra help – I don't think many people knew what dyslexia was at the time, though I had heard something about it by chance on a radio show.

I devised my own ways to help me study. I taught myself to listen as much as possible in class. Sometimes this didn't help because I immediately forgot what someone had said. When I did remember, I went home and wrote down everything, adding some extra notes in my own words. We were told to write in our own words to help us understand what we were being taught, and that helped things make sense to me.

Top Tip from Jenny: When I studied for exams, I wrote out what I was trying to remember on different sheets of paper and kept the number of words on each sheet as small as possible. I knew if I wrote too much, I would forget everything.

When I left university, I started work at a radio station as a studio assistant. My main role there was to be given a script with information about a product or service that I would sell to the listeners by reading out loud from the paper. I wasn't meant to make it obvious I was reading, because it would sound like I didn't know what I was talking about.

I couldn't have been given a trickier role. Even if I'd seen the script before it would have looked brand new to me. My anxiety became too bad and eventually I was laid off.

My feelings were so low. I contacted Dyslexia Nigeria and Dr Adrienne Tikolo, the Managing Director, invited me to see her for a free dyslexia assessment. She suggested I come to the office to help. I could prove to myself that I could do a good job.

I have never left!

I work in the communications department. What I love most about this work is the impact we make. Nigeria is a very academic country. You have to be able to do certain things at a certain age, and if you cannot you're considered lazy, stupid, or dumb. You're seen as someone who can't make it in life. Quite a number of people in Nigeria believe that dyslexia is an excuse, just another label that doesn't make any sense.

It's such a joy to explain to parents about their children's difficulties and to see the relief on their faces or hear it in their voice when they finally understand what's happening with their child. I tell them about some symptoms of dyslexia, and they say, 'Wait. How do you know that is exactly what happens?'

This helps take away their feelings of uncertainty and gives them some direction. They learn how to support their child, get back their self-esteem, and know they can achieve anything in their life.

A New Path

When I left the radio station, I had felt lost. This took me back to my feelings at school where nothing made sense to me. Working at Dyslexia Nigeria gave me a path to follow. I've acquired new skills and developed my capacity to help others, all thanks to Dr Tikolo.

I am usually the first point of contact for anyone getting more information about our services. I'm the one a caller speaks with or who responds to their emails. I'm also often in charge of the social media platforms.

Even though I struggled to learn in school, I learn so much in my day-to-day life now. I think this is because my work is a lot more practical. It involves a lot more than just having to sit down and listen to somebody talk and take notes. I am doing what I've been taught, and this helps me remember.

Making Me Stronger

I think everything I have experienced because I have dyslexia helps me at work. It has made me resilient. It has pushed me to lengths that I didn't think I could go to. There are still times when I think, 'I can't do this anymore', but then I think, 'Well, you've got this far. There's no need to stop now'.

I can easily understand when someone is having a difficult time with dyslexia or anything else. I know what that looks like. I know the demeanour, the body language. I've been there way too many times.

I believe dyslexia has made me a kind person – I've been told that. I'm also quite a trustworthy friend. If I ever hurt my friends' feelings, they tell me that they know it wasn't intentional. I'm someone who's sensitive in my relationships. I think dyslexia makes them better.

Although I'm quite quiet, people say I'm a good communicator. In the past I've been quite withdrawn. This is a lot to do with coping without any form of support in the early days. I had to find a way to be by myself and enjoy my own company and not be around people. Sometimes still now people want to talk and talk and talk and I don't really enjoy that. Even if the communication is online, it takes me a long time to send my words back to someone.

Reading, writing, and spelling are still weaknesses for me. Of course, there is tons of AI and assistive technologies these days that help. I cannot live without Grammarly.

Top Tip from Jenny: When I was a lot younger, I used to call a friend and say, 'Spell biscuit'. Now I don't need to call anyone. I found out that Google has this microphone and all you have to do is just tap on it and then say the word you want and then it will bring up the spelling and a definition for you. These things help, but don't take away from the fact that I still struggle if I don't have them.

What's important is that we do our best to believe in ourselves, and we take this one day at a time. Looking too much at the big picture might overwhelm us. Dyslexia affects people differently, so I do whatever works for me and that may not work for you. Many of us will have experienced negative words, piercing words, that were said to us when we were younger. These can stop us from doing what we're good at. Just remember, it's just their opinion of you, it is not the outcome of who you will become. You can do this!

Motivational words can't have an effect unless you push yourself. The action must come from you. Just remembering the way I felt at school and how it affected everything in my life means that I don't want to go back there. That is motivation enough for me and helps me to keep pushing. Also I don't want to disappoint my mother or let her down. I want to make her proud. Dr Tikolo has supported me, too, and I don't want to let her down either. She has held me up, drawing me out of whatever hole I might have fallen into.

If you're supporting someone with dyslexia, my advice to you would be to be extremely patient. Big changes are not going to happen in a day or a week or a month. Don't put anyone you're helping under pressure or give them the feeling that they must do something within a certain period of time. This would make things worse. Space and time is what we need, and that has definitely worked for me.

Learning can happen without any pressures, when you may not even know you're being taught something.

The Importance of Kindness

Kindness helps a lot because that's not something that people with dyslexia experience enough. Much of what we face is the opposite.

I am so much happier not being at school. I think this is because I don't see the people who made me feel unworthy. I don't have to do things that I don't want to do or don't understand. I don't have to be in an environment with a group of people learning something that I didn't get yesterday, so I'm not sure why it's being taught the same way today.

I had no idea at school that I'd be doing what I'm doing now and enjoying it so much. If I pictured myself, it was usually going downwards.

So for anyone finding things difficult now, please try to take in that it's not the end of the world. You may feel like you don't have a place and might not be able to contribute now, but it's not always going to be like that. Feelings of inadequacy because of what happens in school can change when we leave.

Some people have the same pressures, unkind words, and insults at home, but if you don't it is easier to leave school behind. Just don't give up in any way. And if you know people who seem to have life figured out, hang round them a lot. They may help you navigate through difficult times.

Whatever you decide to do after school, let it be something you enjoy. You'll be expected to do a lot of things in a short period of time, with a different pace. If you like what you're doing on a day when things are going downhill, you still have the energy to wake up the next day and go for it again. I know with my job that if I help just one person, I feel my day is worthwhile.

"Motivational words from others can't have an effect unless you push yourself. The action must come from you. Just remembering the way I felt at school and how it affected everything in my life means that I don't want to go back there. That is motivation enough for me. It helps me to keep pushing."

JARRED, 21, ARUBA, THE CARIBBEAN/ THE HAGUE, THE NETHERLANDS

“At the footwear company I’ve learnt that if you have someone to support you at the beginning, you can work independently, and your skills can fly.”

High school was tough and boring. You had to take subjects even if you didn’t like them. I felt stuck there and couldn’t chase what I was passionate about.

I left when I was 16 and spent three years at culinary art school in my home island in the Caribbean, learning how to be a professional chef. Then I came to the Netherlands to study graphic design, and I’m just finishing my degree.

It’s so important to focus on areas that interest you. As well as graphic design, I’m a tattoo artist. I’ve been doing that for two years, and the two lines of work go well with each other.

I’m also doing an internship for a footwear company, creating all their newsletters, and doing their Instagram posts and website work, and I love that.

When I finish my degree, my aim is to keep working at the same footwear company. I previously had an internship at another company, and it went wrong. They told me someone would guide me through the processes of making graphic work for them, but no one helped at all. They held back my graphic design skills, and I couldn’t flourish.

At the footwear company I've learnt that if you have someone to support you at the beginning, you can then work independently, and your skills can fly.

When I was studying at school, my mum helped me for hours every day. I don't know how far I would have come without her. The school I went to said they would help but they fooled us. We tried to find a tutor, but they were expensive, and they didn't work out. Mum knew how to help me because she understood me.

Then at culinary school, I worked hard independently and achieved the highest grades. It was like my mum had given me this push and then I could achieve by myself, which was great.

Top Tip from Jarred: By the time I was at cookery school I realized that if I read a sentence more than three times it would get stuck in my head. I learnt to write words correctly, though it was still a process to do that.

At school no one knew how much work I put into a test. I don't think my friends knew. If I tried to tell them, 'Hey, I have dyslexia, it means this', or, 'It means that', people just saw it as laziness or an excuse.

Now, looking back, I see my time at school has taught me that when I face challenges, I must have the motivation not to quit early on. That's an important lesson.

Some of what I was taught in biology and history and

other subjects was interesting, and I'm pleased I did that learning, though I don't use any of this in my work now.

I've done most of my learning not at school or college but using YouTube. I love to see documentaries and be informed about things that people don't normally talk about. These can be random things like a fact about Africa or details about a war somewhere. I educate myself.

Thanks to dyslexia, I see things in a different way. I notice that when I talk to certain people, I have a different viewpoint. It's like I see in different angles, or I've already thought about an issue in other ways. Most people say, 'It's just like this', but there can be way more sides to something.

I strive for success. I work hard for it. I'd say to anyone, don't limit yourself and fight for what you want. It's a cruel world sometimes, but you need to keep going.

One of the reasons I'm successful is because of the influence of my parents. When I was younger, we weren't poor, but we weren't middle class either. I saw my parents fighting hard to get to where they got to.

They now own their own business. I gained my motivation from them because they did so much for me. My parents used some of the fighting power they have to help me. That makes me want to reach higher for myself.

My dad is a great role model because he is dyslexic. We have the same drive for entrepreneurial success. I do graphic design work for him as well, so I do multiple jobs

at the same time. Sometimes I work after work. I want to get far in my life, and I don't want to be an average Joe.

Dyslexia still affects me of course. I forget a lot of stuff, so I have to write everything down on note planning on my phone. On social media, I mostly use Instagram, which is visual.

Anyone wanting to support someone with dyslexia needs to have patience. No one can help that we think in a certain way. Do a little research, and don't assume you know things because of what you've heard from other people.

If you're at school now and you're struggling, don't give up. I know that's easy to say, but keep going. Find a passion and that will make you work harder to do well. Life is so much better since I left school. I'm happier. I'm doing something I want to do. I can put my skills and the benefits I get from dyslexia to good use. You can too.

> **"I strive for success. I work hard for it. I'd say to anyone, don't limit yourself and fight for what you want. It's a cruel world sometimes, but you need to keep going."**

HELENA, 24, LONDON, ENGLAND

> “Being in a different country gave me some kind of freedom. I was with all these people who were more worried than I was about their English. It felt great being in a place where I developed my confidence and didn’t need to be completely grammatically correct.”

Growing up with parents who aren’t English was confusing for me. My older sister spoke Turkish, Italian, and English when she was younger. I didn’t speak at all. I finally started talking when I was about five and I felt super-puzzled about what language to use.

After I left school, I thought I would do an art foundation course, but first I visited a friend at university in Amsterdam. While I was there, I went to the open day of her uni, decided to apply, took an exam, and was given a place.

Being in a different country gave me some kind of freedom. I was with all these people who were more worried than I was about their English. I was the one reassuring them: ‘Oh, I understand you. You’re completely fine’. It felt great being in a place where I developed my confidence and didn’t need to be completely grammatically correct.

I ended up doing an art degree and staying there for five years, which was amazing. In the UK, the universities I visited seemed to be more like machines, less personal, getting people in who suit them and making them all the same. They had lost their community vibe, but it was still there in Amsterdam.

Looking back to school, those times were difficult for me. I always felt a bit behind. I always had this feeling that I was second guessing whether I had understood something.

What would take someone else half an hour would take me three hours, with Mum sitting with me explaining things. I was not an easy child. I would get so frustrated. I couldn't communicate with my mum, and she was just trying to help me. I had some teachers who were supportive who saw that I was completely fine in class, but not in exam situations when I didn't understand anything. I couldn't link what was in my head and what the question was asking me.

I loved university straightaway. When we had an essay assignment, I realized it didn't matter how they were written or structured. They were more about trying to get us to express ourselves. It was liberating.

In Amsterdam we used quite basic language but managed to have deep conversations and connect well with each other. We didn't use the harder vocabulary that a lot of people wouldn't know.

I finished in July. I'm applying to do art residencies, where they give you accommodation and you work towards creating an exhibition. I specialize in video art, writing, and performance art. Over the past six months, I worked in a bar in London to make enough money to travel and I'm now in Argentina and then Peru. I've been working in restaurant kitchens for the past five years, so I find that work pretty easy. I'm quite good socially and it's one of the ways I learn well.

Looking at Life Differently

When you tell people you've been to art school, it sounds like that isn't really work, but I do think studying art makes you look at life quite differently. I feel quite disconnected from everything I learnt before. A lot of that was mandatory, learning things because I had to.

I think most dyslexic people just think differently. We see situations from another perspective. I will come at ideas from a completely opposite angle. That fits in with my life at university. They taught us how to think for ourselves. Why am I making certain decisions? What will I do if it's not working? They taught me that if I put my mind to doing something, I can do it. I have left with such a positive attitude.

> **Top Tip from Helena:** Still now if I have to write things I change the colour of the page I'm writing on to an off yellow or green. I start essays just by writing down a reference list of all the thoughts I have, so that I have the list to add in later and I can develop my ideas further on. I'm not worried about getting something perfect the first time round, as I was at school. In those days I wouldn't write anything down until it was perfect, and it would never be perfect because I was struggling.

Top Tip from Helena: Since I was a kid, I've been a big audio book listener, sometimes as well as having the physical book with me, so I can listen while I read. I also colour co-ordinated all my notes for school exams, and highlighting helped. I don't have a photographic memory, but I could sometimes remember if a certain colour was in a certain place, and that I wrote these facts in that colour.

I do a lot of social media, posting films. We have our phones and computers correcting our spelling all the time, so in my head I'm not bad at spelling, but I don't know if that's true.

I think for a while I was embarrassed or ashamed of being dyslexic. Now I'm like it's not that we are any less than others, it's just that we do things a bit differently. If it's something that stresses you out, just tell people, 'I may do things differently, but I can still get them to you on time'.

If you have dyslexia, there's nothing you can't do if you put your mind to it. You can. Just keep going.

"I think most dyslexic people just think differently. We see situations from another perspective. I will come at ideas from a completely opposite angle. That fits in with my life at university. They taught us how to think for ourselves. Why am I making certain decisions? What will I do if it's not working? They taught me that if I put my mind to doing something, I can do it. I have left with such a positive attitude."

CHAPTER 6

How Dyslexia Helps Me Now

FIN FORSYTH @FINFO.R

EVELYNE, 25, COUNTY WICKLOW, IRELAND

> **"When I look back, I see how limited I was by school. There was so much emphasis on academics, who's the best, who's the worst. I felt deflated and stressed. The whole day was a reminder of what I wasn't good at. Once I left, I just took off!"**

All these years on, I still have the odd nightmare about school. I'll wake up in a bit of a sweat after a dream that I've been in English class. Then I realize it was a dream and the relief is overwhelming.

When I look back, I see how limited I was by school. There was so much emphasis on academics, who's the best, who's the worst. I felt deflated and stressed. The whole day was a reminder of what I wasn't good at.

Once I left, I just took off!

The feeling was almost instant. I knew this was going to be the start of my new life. I thought, 'I'm on my own now, and I'm going to do what I want'. I knew it was going to be better.

It hit me that school meant only getting measured in one area, the area I happened not to be good in. The other parts of me never had a chance to shine.

When I knew that I wanted to be a nurse, I told someone

on the school staff what I was planning. She told me not to bother and that I wouldn't get in.

So that was a bit of a kick in the teeth.

Luckily, I'm quite headstrong. If I have my eye on something, it's going to happen, and I didn't listen to her. Through blood, sweat, and tears, I ended up doing OK at school. We have a disability access route in Ireland, which means they gave me a little bit of grace on how many points I gained in my leaving certificate. If you don't quite get to the mark, there are a certain number of places for people who have something like dyslexia, dyspraxia, or ADHD.

So I went straight to Dublin City University to study nursing, which was a bit of a shock. I was a bit floored with the essays and all the citations – the way you have to back every single point you make by scouring through journals and other people's essays. All that reading was too much for me. One good thing was that we wrote everything on the computer so there was no more writing on paper.

Also, my university was amazing. They made everything easier, giving me extra time for assignments, extra time in exams, my own room to take exams in, my own laptop. It was unreal.

I came out with a first, which shocked me. I think one good thing was that about a quarter of the final grade came from your results for hands-on nursing. From the start I gave my all to the practical side. I immediately felt I was good at that, and I hoped that would make up for the other areas.

Helping Others

After I graduated, I specialized in nursing people with different kinds of intellectual disabilities like Down syndrome and autism. I learnt different kinds of special techniques that helped in this work. I think my struggles at school had influenced me to follow this path, and it has always been in my personality to help other people.

> **Top Tip from Evelyne:** I love my work, but sometimes it's hard to hide the difficulties I have. There's a lot of paperwork and not a lot of room for error. If you have dyslexia, you do have to put a lot more focus into what you're doing, and concentrate. It's hard to multitask sometimes, so if I'm writing away and someone's talking, I have to say, 'Please stop talking to me, or I'm going to end up writing all sorts'.

One place I don't worry about spelling is on social media. Everything's emojis and I love a few emojis. I caption 99 per cent of my Instagram with emojis. Take what you want from that.

Generally my life is going well. I just signed on my first property, and I never thought that would happen. I know other people who were doing better than me in school aren't there yet, and that's OK as well. One thing I've learnt is that we're all on a journey and we all get there at different times.

I learn in all different ways. I have a nephew who's two in September and he's opened my eyes about what's important. He and the people I work with have helped me take a step back and say to myself, 'I can walk, I can talk, I can do all these things that other people can't do. Isn't that something to be grateful for?' I learnt to have more appreciation for basic stuff that we take for granted. A huge life lesson.

Since school I've learnt how to communicate with people and to be more open to different cultures and different abilities. I think dyslexia affected my friendships in school when we weren't as mature. We were all conditioned to be competing against each other. As you get older your friendships are based on real connection. I can't even remember what marks I was given at school now. That's how unimportant it all is.

I know now it's not important to think how well I'm doing, but to be able to go home and say to myself, 'Everybody's happy. Everybody's looked after'. I've been influenced by the friends I met at university and in my job who just accept you for who you are. It's no longer about how smart you are or how well you did in school. That doesn't matter anymore. What matters is that you're a decent person.

Life has taught me about harnessing the strong parts of your abilities, whether that's being empathetic, being an extrovert, whatever it is. You don't have to be smart on paper, you can be smart in kindness, you can be smart in other areas. Intelligence is not just an A plus, it's how you treat people.

> **Top Tip from Evelyne:** Everyone should know they are intelligent in their own way. You need to find the parts of you that are strong and put them to work in whatever career you go into. Don't listen to anybody telling you what you should be doing. Harness what you have. That's why we have all these different jobs and different talents. Have faith in yourself, and faith in your future self as well. The best thing you can do is to figure out exactly what your strong points are. What you can do, not what you can't.

When you have dyslexia, you learn to put the graft in. That's the way I commit to things, because they don't come easily to me. I've transferred that to other areas of my life as well, like my job and my family and now my property. I've learnt to become a hard worker. I notice things on a deeper level, even small details. I see the world in a different way.

If you can get support, then take it because you do need it. Just like the saying that says it takes a village to raise a child, it can take a village to get us over the line.

If you're supporting someone with dyslexia, you need a lot of compassion and understanding. You need a lot of patience. Dyslexia is actually very hard to deal with, especially if you don't have a lot of support at school or home.

After school, life gets better, so much better. When you get there you're going to see it for yourself. It's hard to have confidence and self-belief when you feel left behind, but with hard work and a bit of struggle you're going to be better off. You'll walk out of there stronger and more resilient. You're not going to believe what's coming your way.

> **"Life has taught me about harnessing the strong parts of your abilities, whether that's being empathetic, being an extrovert, whatever it is. You don't have to be smart on paper, you can be smart in kindness, you can be smart in other areas. Intelligence is not just an A plus, it's how you treat people."**

DOUG, 16, LONDON, ENGLAND

> **"Cooking is more stressful at college than at home. When I cook at home, they're not going, 'You need to tweak the seasoning'. I can also make my family less complicated dishes like scrambled eggs or an omelette. At college there's more of a noisy kitchen setting, but I do enjoy it."**

When I was young, I thought about being a chef, but then I didn't think about it again for a long while. I had done a lot of baking with my mum when I was small and took cakes into school to raise money for events there. After that I went to some children's camps with my dad where I had to cook for big groups of people and that didn't worry me at all. I found it easy working out how to do meals for large numbers and solving any problems we found.

Then I went on a couple of cookery courses when I was 13 or 14 and I enjoyed these. After this I decided to apply for catering college after school.

For me school was mainly about the friends I hung out with. When it came to the lessons, some were OK, like photography and design technology, and I passed maths. I studied food tech and did OK on the cooking side, but I did badly on the coursework as it just wouldn't go into my brain. In English and pretty much every other subject I didn't do well at all. I'm still having to retake English now and I have an English lesson every Friday.

I was aware it was a struggle for me to do my schoolwork compared with other people. I still can't write very well, though my reading is OK.

At school I got distracted very easily. I don't think what I learnt there helped me much at all. I think I could barely read in Year 7,* but Billy, who taught me *Toe by Toe*** when I was younger, became my tutor. He came to my house twice a week for an hour and this really helped.

> **Top Tip from Doug:** The more someone knows you, the more they understand your dyslexia. My dyslexia confused some people when they were trying to help. I might know the word but not know what it was when it was written down. Billy knew every time what I meant. It was good that I had the same tutor for the whole time, and that I knew and liked him.

I needed Billy's help because at secondary school I didn't get much individual help.

Something that distracted me a lot at school was noise. When I have people around me, I can't focus. If I'm in a laptop class and all these other laptops are going clack clack clack that disturbs me too.

I think I'm learning a lot more now I'm not in that teaching setting you have at school. At college, the

---

* Ages 11–12 in the UK

** A highly structured phonics-based teaching manual

teachers aren't actual teachers. They're chefs who want to teach. This means I don't feel like a student as much.

At catering college there's only a little bit of writing, and the writing we do is nothing about spelling. Sometimes I have to explain to the teachers what I've written, but that's the only problem. Pretty much the rest of the time I just cook, at least for four hours. I prefer the cooking to the front of house stuff like waiting on tables, because there is no writing when you cook, no need to take down people's orders.

Cooking is more stressful at college than at home. When I cook at home, they're not going, 'You need to tweak the seasoning'. I can also make my family less complicated dishes like scrambled eggs or an omelette. At college there's more of a noisy kitchen setting, but I do enjoy it. I serve my dish to the teacher, though quite often what I've made has complicated names in French that I can't remember.

Gordon Ramsay visited our catering college a week after we started. It was exciting. He talked about how he grew up in the chef world, and how he thinks it's going to gradually become a less stressful industry. The other exciting thing I've done with the college is travel to India to learn about different Indian food.

Maths and Cooking

The maths I learnt at school is pretty much the only thing from school that's gone into my head. There's lots of maths in cooking. It's all millilitres and milligrams and stuff like that. Sometimes you get dishes from other countries and they're in the wrong measurements and you have to know how to change them. I use fractions and percentages and that doesn't scare me.

I think dyslexia helps me with cooking because I'm more of a creative person. I'm someone who's at home using my hands. It helps me that I know when my cooking is instinctively right. When it comes to making sure food looks good, some in my class are better than me, but I do enjoy it.

Quite often we do a week of safety tests, and I find them very irritating. Suddenly, I need to revise and I'm not so good at that. The tests might be about fire safety, or which chopping boards are for which foods – you have different coloured chopping boards for meat, bread, and fish and you can't mix them up. Or the test might be about what all the different knives are called, when some of them look really similar. After revising I find I know all the words, but I can't match the words in my head with what's in front of me. Sometimes this bothers me a lot.

This might not surprise them as I told them when I came to the catering college for my interview that I have dyslexia, and they said a lot of people there do.

Something that helps me is that I'm quite friendly, and the more people know you, the easier it is in class. You have to ask around a lot, because it's irritating when someone has an ingredient that you want that is being passed round the classroom.

My friends all know I have dyslexia, and they know I can read, but they know that writing is not my best thing. Some of them take my phone and write Instagram posts for me, though I don't do much Instagram now. I text some of my friends, but besides that I would rather ring someone up than text them. They're used to me.

My mum has supported me an awful lot, but now she supports me sometimes more than I want her to. At school she emailed my teachers if I didn't understand something, and they sent information to help. Sometimes she still emails my teachers, and I don't need that now. I have told her this many times.

I think something people need to understand is that dyslexia is not just about writing and reading. That always catches people out. It's also about forgetting things. My dad puts something in my room and asks me to put it in the cupboard and I'll say yes. Once he leaves the room whatever he said has gone out of my mind. It was the same in school. I learnt my times tables and the next morning I couldn't remember anything from the night before.

Typing has helped me along. I'm just much faster at typing than writing. I can use the delete button and it has Autocorrect. Billy was able to find this app you download on computers. When you want to read something, it puts just one word at a time on the screen. You press play and the next word comes up. Without this I get caught on words sometimes.

I feel like I now have a reason to study and a reason to

do the work I'm asked to do. If it's something I need to know, like how to julienne a carrot, I'm completely there. I can concentrate easily if what's being taught is connected to my real life.

I see my future in cooking. There's a chance I'll do an apprenticeship in a year or so and that would be working for four days and going to college for the last day. Eventually I want to be in some kind of professional high-class restaurant, maybe Michelin star, but not forever because I know people get burnt out. Maybe, after that, I'd just like to bake.

> "I think dyslexia helps me with cooking because I'm more of a creative person. I'm someone who's at home using my hands. It helps me that I know when my cooking is instinctively right."

LOLA, 26, LONDON, ENGLAND

"Remember how many options there are. There are endless business ideas. There are so many online courses to take if you want to build up knowledge in a particular area. Fill your brain with that."

When I was 18, after school and college, I decided university wasn't for me. Instead, I created a business plan for my own footwear brand. I did a course with The Prince's Trust,* the charity which helps young people starting businesses. I remember on the first day thinking, 'I've learnt more today than I did the whole time I was at school.'

They taught us everything about running a business, from finances to marketing. They held workshops and connected us to people relevant to the sector we were going into. Then I pitched my business plan to them and was accepted. I received a loan to start my company and they gave me a mentor to give me extra help that I needed.

Then a school friend whose family worked in the industry said he could introduce me to the region of China that specializes in manufacturing footwear. I went out to China and networked and found the best supplier for the boots and shoes I had designed and the quantities I needed, and I began to order samples.

* This is the charity set up by King Charles when he was Prince of Wales to help young people. It is now known as The King's Trust.

Once I was happy with the samples, I placed my first orders. I created a website to sell them and marketed them on Instagram.

The company did well for a couple of years, with sales going well and celebrities wearing my brand, though bigger companies sometimes stole my designs, which was annoying.

All the time I was learning. I was incredibly careful about my English in all my communications. Every Instagram post and every email to a customer had to be written perfectly. That was great training for me, as my spelling was terrible. I also impressed myself with my maths. I thought I would never need to use maths again after I left school, because I saw myself as a creative person, but I was completely wrong. I used it every day and still do.

Although the company did well and the sales peaked, the money I made wasn't enough to make a full-time living. I also found it quite difficult working by myself in my bedroom.

Then I saw an advert for a company that wanted a teenager to help with some paperwork over the summer.

I applied and found out the company was – by complete chance – fashion designers and suppliers to some of the big brands. I joined them on a placement for a few weeks, helping out with couriers, garment steaming, and other small jobs.

I loved it. I was absorbing the details of every tiny task

that was given to me. I tried to do the very best I could at every stage to show my work ethic. I even used some of my knowledge I had from setting up the footwear supply chain.

They ended up keeping me on, and I was made office assistant. I've been there for six years and I've been promoted to assistant account manager, account manager, senior account manager, and now I'm the sales director.

Dyslexic Talents

I still love it there. I feel it uses my talents, and so many of them I put down to dyslexia.

Every day there are problems along the supply chain that need resolving. So even though the work can be stressful, it's never boring. There can be countless problems throughout the day. People will call and ask my opinion. I have to think quickly and in that moment give my advice, or discuss my thoughts with someone else.

While my work is stimulating, I miss not using the creative side of my brain more. I want to bring that creative element back into my life, maybe by starting to sketch or paint again, or launching a side hustle.

One part of my work that is more creative is attending design meetings with the design teams and the buyers, where everyone discusses current trends. It's a creative space, even though I'm not the one designing. We look

at catwalk shows, new samples, sketches, and prints. That's a fun part of the job.

The most rewarding part is placing orders. I love that feeling, knowing that I'm achieving well for the company and knowing other people know that too.

Thinking back to school, I don't think there was much I liked about it, apart from specific classes like art and photography. I was careful to invest my time in those subjects that I thought would help me in my future, as well as gaining experience out of school where possible. I recommend that.

I do think it helps to pay attention in maths because in my job now I need to have a maths brain. Sometimes in meetings I need to do calculations on the spot.

Triple Checking Everything

At work I triple check everything, all maths and English, to make sure it's right. I don't want to make silly mistakes. My spelling is bad. I use Spellcheck, and if Spellcheck doesn't work because I've spelt something too wrong, I ask whoever's sitting next to me.

I don't know where I learnt this, but I do enjoy structuring an email properly to get a point across. It's my job to be the clearest communicator possible. My reading is poor and I need to read emails over and over and over to make sure I'm not missing a point or a detail. Luckily I always find it easier to read something I'm interested in. Otherwise the words are too overwhelming.

I don't know if this is down to dyslexia, but my timekeeping is not good – though I'm on time for work – and my memory is definitely not good. I keep forgetting the questions I'm being asked in this interview! If my colleague reads me out something and I want to make a change to it, I'll have to keep asking her to read it from the beginning because I won't be able to remember any of it.

Top Tip from Lola: The advice I would give anyone is to go for a career which is in line with what you love. This will sound obvious, but we only get one life. We have to work most of the week. Once you're there, go the extra mile. I never have the mindset of finishing bang on five. I would rather do my job the best I possibly can and give my future self the best chance of progressing.

My mum has made sure I feel positive about having dyslexia. It has so many pluses for me. Learning about your strengths and weaknesses is so important. Then you can find ways to get support for your weaknesses and focus on your strengths. I was always so into art and photography and that made me feel good about myself. I was pretty sure I would leave the other subjects behind. In fact, maths ended up coming with me. I remember all those endless lessons in science and English and how my brain could only take in a certain amount. There wasn't space for the information to soak in.

Life after school is so much better. It's a time to be professional, to work hard, to keep the best relationships possible with your colleagues, and be a good listener. If your boss is correcting you, or thinks you should have done something differently, then be open-minded to that. And don't be shy about voicing your opinions.

I know some people go to uni and come out still not knowing what they want to do. Just remember how many options there are. There are endless business ideas. There are so many online courses to take if you want to build up knowledge in a particular area. Fill your brain with that. There's no need to go to university straight after school. I know people who've gone in their mid-20s, so there's nobody to tell you what order you should do things. Just follow your passions, build your CV, and have confidence in yourself.

"Life after school is a time to be professional, to work hard, to keep the best relationships possible with your colleagues, and be a good listener. If your boss is correcting you, or thinks you should have done something differently, then be open-minded to that. And don't be shy about voicing your opinions."

NICK, 26, BEDFORD, ENGLAND

"At school because I was dyslexic, everything took extra effort. Now my goal is to make everything easier."

After school, I went to university to do Politics, Philosophy, and Economics. It seemed like a degree that would serve me well, although at this point I was completely out of touch with what I might want to do in life.

For my sixth form* I had left my state school and joined a private school where the attitude was you had to go to university when you left. It would be ridiculous to think about anything else. I remember that if there were some students who had that textbook entrepreneur's disposition and personality, people would take the piss out of them. The prevailing attitude seemed to be, 'Oh, this guy thinks he's going to change the world. Just go to uni, mate!'

Coming out of university I don't think I had any sense of where I wanted to go. I was in a less-than-ideal state of mind. I had broken up with a girlfriend and things weren't going super well for me. I don't think I had any clue about what I wanted to do.

A lot of my uni mates were off to do postgrad work

* When you are 17 and 18 in the UK

schemes in London and I was a bit jealous of them. I felt obliged to do the same.

Then my dad started talking to me about a business idea he was developing. My mum and dad were both born in Malawi where our grandparents and great grandparents had lived. They have always had strong links with the place. Working with his father, Dad learnt about the benefits of growing macadamia nut trees in Malawi. They are a great way for elderly people there to have a pension, as they are easier to gather than a crop in a field. In a developing country like Malawi, this could have a huge impact.

The trees are also great for the environment. Recently, Malawi has had three cyclones and two droughts in four years. There are a lot of environmental problems, and these trees have the potential to help restore the country's denuded landscape.

Finally, Dad made the decision to set up a company called Nutcellars,* to help people in Malawi access international markets, sell the macadamias for a fair price, and benefit the country where he was born. He asked my brother and me to work with him. He was keen. This was about intergenerational goals, inherited dreams.

I was less convinced. I told him, 'I'll give you two years.'

I didn't know what I wanted to do with my life, but I hadn't thought it was selling macadamia nuts.

* www.nutcellars.com

It's now been coming up to five years. I've found that I love working with my family on something I really care about. It's made me realize that by comparison I hadn't cared about my degree at all.

School and university both raised issues that hadn't left me feeling good about myself. It was the workload. I remember some university exams were literally back-to-back. I failed one of them, which led to a period of uncertainty that had a big impact on my mental health. Since then I have been able to rediscover a feeling of competence and self-belief.

Wasting Time

When I started working at Nutcellars, I was big on procrastination, which is what used to happen when I didn't have an imminent deadline. At the time, I didn't feel productive or fulfilled. I didn't have a sense of what this company was going to be. It was my dad's vision, and my brother Tim had a clear-cut role with his marketing background. I didn't know what I could meaningfully contribute. I wasted a lot of time on tasks that didn't feel important, thinking, 'I don't need to do this now. I can do it later'.

We started up the business just before Covid hit. This meant that, because of the pandemic, we had stock with a sell by date and no market to sell it through, as all the restaurants and pubs were shut. This could have been a disaster.

It was then I found out that work suits me in a way that

the education system didn't. I had to get in-the-zone and start selling. Farmers markets were the answer in those early times. It was hard graft, but I found out I was good at talking to people. It was all about generating a good feeling between myself and the customer first, and not rushing to find a way to funnel conversations towards the sale. I was proud of that. I focused on developing this skillset. I spent a lot of time listening to audiobooks – *How to Make Friends and Influence People*, that kind of thing.

Something shifted inside me. I thought, 'Come on, you can't afford to mess about anymore. Your family needs you'. This turned into the driving motivation in my life, and it was a transformative time. We were working together as a team, bouncing off each other well. We developed a hive mind.

The three of us have achieved so much. The macadamia growers are organized into Fairtrade smallholder farming co-operatives to guarantee they receive more money for their work. The sales are going well, and supermarkets are beginning to stock our products. We've scaled up well as a company and we're ready to scale up further. It's an exciting time for the business and the farmers we work with.

We have created different products, including chocolate-coated macadamias, cinnamon caramelized nuts, and nut butters and spreads. I designed the packaging and I'm proud of that.

The way things have worked out, I'm the operations guy. Much of my work is researching, incorporating, and sometimes making the systems we use to scale as a business. I've also really developed my graphics skills. As a child, I was always a doodler, and I then moved on to Word Art on Microsoft Word and Excel. I didn't value the skill I had in art and dropped it during school. Since working for Nutcellars, I'm now using the whole Adobe suite of programs to develop our brand.

I'm so glad for the opportunity to use skills in the workplace that had been dormant in my earlier years.

Much of my job is finding smart ways of getting the tasks we need to do automated or trimmed down using technology. We're so lucky to live in an age that allows me to learn to do this using YouTube videos. I'm our accountant and I run our books, I do our purchase orders and pallet labels, warehouse numbering, barcodes, nutritional information... it's a hodgepodge of work but it all comes under 'systems', and I've learnt almost everything from the internet.

Automation is my fascination, and I've liberated us as a company from a lot of the time-consuming work we were having to do. At school, because I was dyslexic, everything took me extra effort. Now my goal is to make everything easier.

I put in extra hours and work overtime if something can end up taking less effort. Currently I'm teaching myself to do web design. After that, I'm going to teach myself to code. I want to simplify things as much as possible and focus my creative energy on things that can't be simplified and give them my best shot.

As someone with dyslexia I think I see the answer to problems in a very different way from other people. There are things about me that are considered drawbacks, like struggling with reading, as I have that line-by-line thing where everything jumps around. I'm able to compensate, however, by pushing myself in other ways. By doing this, I believe I gain a unique perspective. Any one job at this business here could be draining and I have a thousand of them, so I ask myself constantly what the most efficient way is to do everything.

Top Tip from Nick: When I think about school and university now, I think they are times for anyone with dyslexia to be patient. Educational institutions have a generalized approach for educating the mainstream, but as we're on the fringes, all we can do is our best.

It's possible to get creative with the challenges we face, and we can take advantage of any opportunity school gives us, but also remember that school is a pre-game to life – it's not what life is about. Teachers are trying their best to teach you, but when you're finally in the working world, find yourself a niche that suits you. These are available in ways at work that are not necessarily available in school.

Life after school is definitely better than life in school, though it was great to be among my friends. I have less time for friendships now because I'm so busy with my work, but if you're pursuing success, that's a choice you make in terms of how you invest your time.

If you have young people you care about with dyslexia, it's important to take extra care to listen and understand them. For those of us with a fringe mind, it can take more time to formulate what you want to say and how to make yourself understood.

Anything Can Be Learnt

We *can* develop a skillset. We *can* learn to do something well and it's important to believe that. My time at the farmers markets and in the years since showed me that anything can be learnt. That's a powerful belief for anyone to have.

There are always workarounds and shortcuts in life. If you don't excel in school, you will find other ways to compensate. You will find other ways to learn. You may have to work harder but you can get there, and in the process you'll gain a rich, unique perspective that the world desperately needs.

> **"School is a pre-game to life – it's not what life is about. Teachers are trying their best to teach you, but when you're finally in the working world, find yourself a niche that suits you. These are available in ways at work that are not necessarily available in school."**

FIN FORSYTH

'Growth and change are a natural part of life. Embracing change allows us to grow stronger, wiser, and more in tune with who we are becoming. Like a tree's seasonal cycles, our shifts are a testament to resilience and renewal.'

@FINFO.R

LEAH, 20, LONDON, ENGLAND

> **“When I was younger I was very shy, and I wouldn’t talk to new people. Working behind the counter in a store really changed me. I saw that talking to people is so important, so it’s not just you in a bubble and everybody else in their bubbles. It’s about interacting and learning from each other.”**

When I was younger, I was very shy. I wouldn’t talk to new people. The most I would say was, ‘Give me a few moments’. It would take me half an hour to start trusting them.

Then I took a job behind the counter at Boots, the chemists, and I had to learn how to talk to everybody. I had so many new experiences, dealing with so many new people I didn’t know. Random people would come in off the street and ask me questions and I’d have to answer them and be respectful. Only one person was horrible, and in the end I said to her, ‘Sorry, I have to serve other customers now’. I found I could even deal with her with confidence.

This changed me and now I can go up to someone and ask them something. I see that talking to people is so important. It’s all about networking, so it’s not just you in a bubble and everybody else in their bubbles. It’s about interacting and learning from each other.

All in the Same Boat

I'm so different from how I was before. I had been so scared to get that first job and scared to go to university, but I found out that everybody is in the same boat. They may not show it so much, but we are all the same.

I'm doing a degree in textile design which is what I wanted to do, but because of my experience at Boots, I think I could have developed a different career. If you stay open to possibilities, you can see where any job can take you. Create a LinkedIn account and start reaching out to different people and places.

Since I left school, my life has become very busy, almost chaotic. I thought things would slow down after A Levels,* but everything is faster. At school we were given 12 weeks to do a unit, but at university it's four weeks. This means I have to produce so much more stuff in a term.

On the other hand, now I'm at university I feel like I'm living life on my time, not on anyone else's. I feel a lot freer. I don't get treated as a child. That's a big step from school to university. Getting things right or wrong is my responsibility. If it's wrong, I've learnt something new for next time.

The great thing is that my designs are going well. School was such a struggle for me, and I'm surprised at how good my life is now.

* A Levels are taken in most of the UK at 18

I don't think I would have managed at school without a tutor to help me. You can't get much one-on-one support in a classroom. I found one of my A Levels difficult because there was so much writing and the teacher didn't understand, so I switched it for photography. But I managed to pass criminology which needed writing just because it was so interesting. I learnt all about juvenile crime and how many who are involved in that have been brought up without a mum or dad before the age of five.

One thing I didn't like about school was sticking to a schedule. I feel like I'm more of a free soul. Towards the end I stopped attending school so much because I was doing my portfolio for university, and school started sending letters home saying if I didn't go, I'd fail, that sort of thing. There weren't many of us applying for art, so I think they didn't understand.

I was quite shocked when I left. I'd been working towards these exams for the past eight years and now it was over. I was never going to go back and be in that environment with those people and the teachers and my friends. I couldn't believe it.

School gave me some general knowledge, but I would say most of my learning happens when I'm out and about, just walking around. I notice the things people are wearing. Sometimes I'll be walking behind someone, thinking, 'Wow, that jumper is hand-knitted. That must have taken 50 hours. I wonder if it's cashmere, alpaca, yak...'

Writing is still a problem for me and I'm going to have to learn to live with that. Overall I think dyslexia helps me now. I'm very creative. I'm someone who thinks creatively while also working quite fast. I need to get my ideas down; I like to see how what I have in my head will turn out. If I like the design, I'll keep it. If not, I'll do it again, changing different components.

The other day I was chatting to someone at dinner, and I told him about one of my ideas. To make sure I didn't forget I started using the receipt from the meal to create what I'd made and show how all the details would work. I wanted to show him how it would come to life.

Someone Will Want Your Work

If you're an artist, you have to keep on putting the work out there to keep showing people what you do. At some stage, somebody will end up being interested or will want to have a conversation with you. If they're not interested it doesn't properly matter. What matters is that you're getting yourself out there in the first place. You're never going to have everyone liking your stuff.

I design in mixed media. I'll do a spray paint on crochet with hand embroidery or machine embroidery. As my subject matter, I use my own story. I'm mixed race with an afro and living in a white community, creating artwork about what's happened to me. My main piece is called Don't Touch My Hair. I've been bullied for my hair in the past and I wanted to empower myself and others who have the same feelings and experiences.

My pictures are 3D and encourage the viewer to touch

them. Different parts have different textures and different dimensions. I'm trying to get them into galleries over here and in the States.

I'm interested in Creative Computing too. This uses conductive wool or wire in knitting samples. You then attach it to an amplifier, and as you stretch the knit in different ways, it makes different sounds and pitches. I think this might be the future.

I have a life plan of doing more education and maybe getting a PhD in textiles, and a bigger life plan of producing and selling work and placing it in all these galleries, creating my stuff in my own studio. That would give me such a buzz.

Build Up Your Future

The person who helped me with my education is my mum. If I couldn't do something and she knew it would help me to be able to learn, she had a way of encouraging me. She'd say, 'You're going to want to have this in the future'. I would be like, 'OK, I should do it'. It was because I knew she wasn't just trying to get me to do something for the sake of it. Two of my mum's older children have dyslexia and they didn't get that much help compared to me. That's why Mum got me loads of help to make sure my dyslexia wouldn't be as significant, in a bad way.

I still struggle in some ways. I can write things on Instagram that look perfectly fine and make sense to me. When I read them the next day, I see they're not even sentences! I don't care about that sort of thing though. Everyone knows I'm dyslexic and it happens. It won't impact me negatively in the end.

Anyone supporting someone with dyslexia shouldn't be over the top. It should be more like, 'If you need any help, just come and ask me'. I still get spellings wrong. I asked my parents how to spell something yesterday and they told me two different ways. It was quite funny, almost like a game.

If you feel like you're struggling, always remember it will get better. Just keep on swimming. In a few years, everything's going to change. You just need to push through the hardest parts of life to get through to the side that's better.

"School gave me some general knowledge, but I would say most of my learning happens when I'm out and about, just walking around. I notice the things people are wearing. Sometimes I'll be walking behind someone, thinking, 'Wow, that jumper is hand-knitted. That must have taken 50 hours. I wonder if it's cashmere, alpaca, yak...'."

ELIJAH, 19, LONDON, ENGLAND

"I never found out how I could fit into the school system, but I think that could have been a blessing in disguise. It's allowed me to be honest and open with myself and explore my creativity."

Leaving school has been good and horrible in different ways. I went from feeling comfortable to feeling lost, feeling trapped to feeling free. One thing has changed – I know dyslexia can't stop me from doing anything.

I believe the educational world forgets about anyone who can't work like a computer. There are all these rules and regulations that you have to battle through. You need to figure out how to function when you're someone who goes against the grain.

I never found out how I could fit into the school system, but I think that could have been a blessing in disguise. It's allowed me to be honest and open with myself and explore my creativity.

I think school taught me the basics of things I had no care for, such as maths and science, but it turns out these subjects aren't useless. They explain most of the workings of the world. It's the teachers who can teach you to love a subject, though, not the curriculum.

Working with Everything Under the Sun

I'm now doing a foundation diploma in sculpture at UAL in London. I'm looking to go into fine art after this. I want to try tattooing, culinary arts, and everything under the sun that's in the art world.

One thing I value is the creative side of dyslexia and that dyslexia helps me to express all the loud noises in my head. I push and push the creativity in me.

It's not all good though. One thing I have always struggled with is organization. This has been true since the day I was born. I was meant to pick my girlfriend up from the airport recently and I left her there. So there's that and forgetting birthdays. It has been tricky at times, but I find honesty tends to fix these problems, and not hiding who you are.

Reading helps me a lot with expressing myself. Although it's horrible, you can find nearly everything you need in the world of books. Something else that helps is not caring what other people think. Why let the world change you? It's when people try to fit themselves into something else that they become less than who they are.

Top Tip from Elijah: I believe people should use everything they feel confused or stupid about to help them express themselves, with the help of a method they have a passion for. Use these difficult feelings to your advantage.

If you're supporting someone with dyslexia, the best thing to do is chill out. Follow their lead and allow them to use their interests to teach them what they need to know and how they can solve things. I had one teacher who didn't make me feel that there was this mountain to climb. It's never any good just talking about someone's faults. Praise them as well. This will humanize you. No one wants to deal with a soulless robot.

Life sometimes feels rocky after school, but it is good to have a path you have created ahead of you. This can sometimes kick you in the shins when you're not looking, but I felt imprisoned at school. It was a claustrophobic feeling like being kept inside a religion I didn't agree with. Having said that, the simplicity of the structure of break time, lunch time, and home time is something I miss.

Leaving school was a big deal for me. Now I've learnt to live on my own. I have a girlfriend and friends from all over the world. I'm living in a wider way.

"One thing I value is the creative side of dyslexia and that dyslexia helps me to express all the loud noises in my head. I push and push the creativity in me."

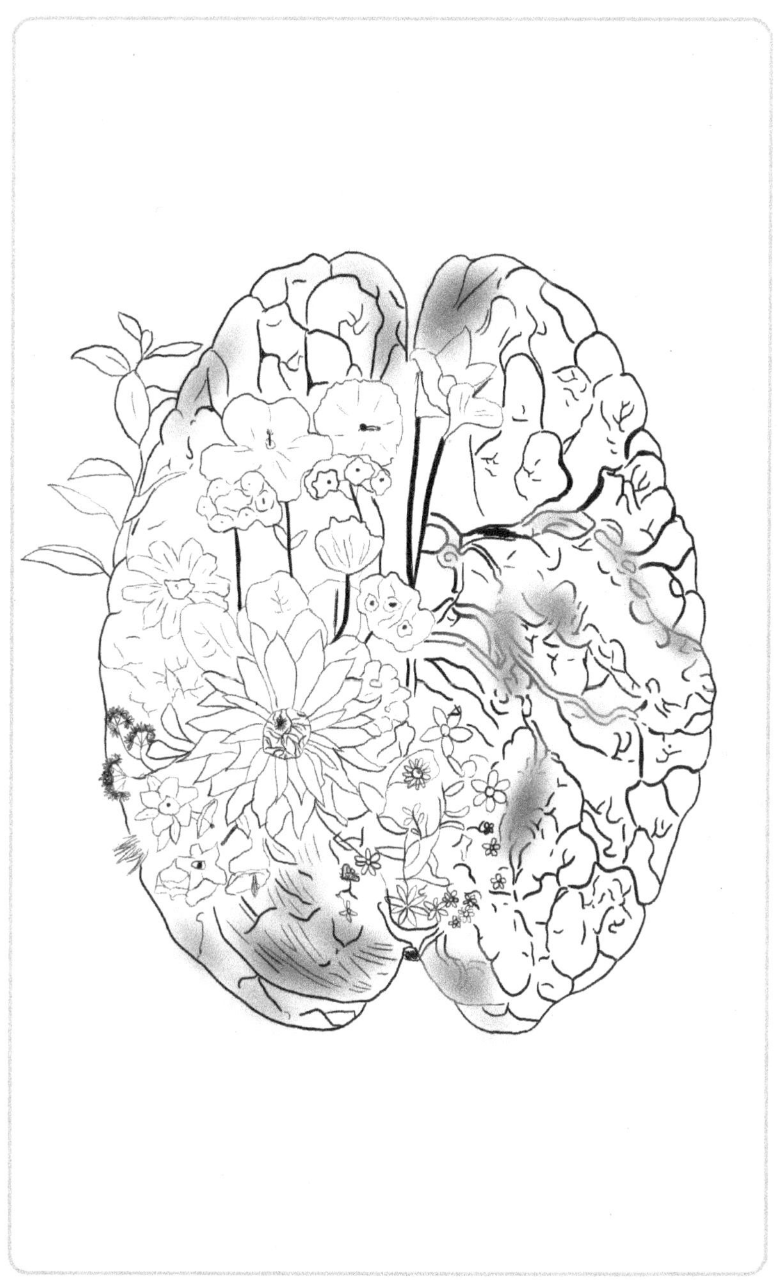

SARAH LONG

CHAPTER 7

Giving Yourself the Best Chance to Succeed

So much links the young people in this book. After school they have progressed with their lives with enthusiasm and creativity, often by taking a path they didn't expect.

They have carried on learning wherever they can – from YouTube, college classes, the working environment, everyday conversations, and what they see as they walk down the street.

They are finding ways to make dyslexia work for them, to help them build strong and inspiring futures. To do this they are working towards their own goals, feeling no need to compare their achievements with those of others.

So many negatives are written and broadcast about teenagers and young people. The stories told in this book show how foolish we would be to underestimate this creative and powerful dyslexic generation.

To guide you towards your own success story, here are some useful ideas.

How to Cope with School as Best You Can

Abby, 18, of Illinois, USA, has just graduated high school where she faced many difficulties with dyslexia, at the same time as dealing with a challenging medical condition.

None of this has stopped her doing well. She has received

an academic scholarship for college, plus another scholarship to play in the college soccer team.

Below she has made some notes to encourage everyone still at high school to do their best and give themselves the biggest chance of a good life after they leave.

- No matter what anyone else says, believe in yourself. No one knows you as well as you do, and no one knows all the ways that you will be able to shine.
- Don't let the things you struggle with pull you down. There is so much more to you.
- If you need extra support, is there anyone at school or outside of school you can approach to help you? I had to spend a year at home when I became sick, but I still did everything I could to get my work done. I had a teacher who helped me at home, and that softened the blow of other teachers who didn't help.
- I decided mindset was everything, taking each day as it comes, rising to each challenge.
- I celebrated the achievements of each day, no matter how big or small. This stopped me feeling sorry for myself.
- Find out what works for you when you study. I rewrite notes in different colours as this helps me remember them – just one example.

- Make sure you have all the accommodations you need. I had extended time for tests. Listening to the teacher is how I learn best, so I was given notes as this meant I didn't need to take my own notes during class.

- Work hard. You will need to work harder than the others :-(

- Think about everyone who is on your side – friends, family, and anyone else. If people make you feel good about yourself, spend time with them.

- Remember, high school is challenging. A lot of hours. If you can get through it, whatever comes next will be different, so keep going. You won't regret it.

And from Abby's brother Cole, 16:

- Don't let dyslexia define who you are. You can do anything you set your mind to, no matter what others might think. Just go for it.

How to Leave High School Feeling as Good as You Can About Yourself

Here are some thoughts from Claire Harvey from the Helen Arkell Dyslexia Charity:*

- A dyslexia assessment will teach you about your

* www.helenarkell.org.uk

areas of weakness, but don't forget to look for your pockets of strength in that report too. You can use your strengths to help you deal with any difficulties you face.

- While you're still at school, seek out ongoing support from teachers who can help you, or organizations like Helen Arkell or your local dyslexia organization.

- If you have had early experiences of feeling you have failed, you may fear tackling new or tricky tasks. You may believe wrongly that you can't do them, and this can increase the learning gap between you and your classmates. You can change how you feel about yourself. When you understand you have areas of strength and you work out how you learn best, you can begin to work out how your efforts will have an impact.

- In our experience, if young people follow a career path into an area that makes best use of their areas of strength, they are likely to enjoy the world of work more and achieve greater job satisfaction and success.

- Moving from the education system to the world of work is an exciting opportunity to practise what you are good at in a job you enjoy, making best use of your unique strengths. If you enjoy dealing with people that's a big clue as to the sort of work that may interest you. If you prefer time on your own, focusing on details, that's another clue.

- We find that young people with dyslexia tend to develop great skills of perseverance and resilience. They know they may need to do things slightly differently, and they know that sometimes tasks take them longer than they take others. Despite this, they tend to stick at the work in hand and keep going.
- Young people with dyslexia also often learn to bounce back from hiccups they face, as they tend to have more experience in this than others. They know how making mistakes can help them learn and grow stronger. This places them in a perfect position to get stronger and develop, no matter what life throws at them.

How to Deal with Change

Change is challenging for all of us, says Janette Beetham, an expert in dyslexia in the workplace.*

She highlights three of the ways we can help ourselves in any situation:

- Gather as much knowledge as possible about the new situation or task you have ahead of you. This can include working out travel details, timetables, and the environment you'll be in. If you write these

* Janette is a Workplace Neurodiversity Consultant and CEO of Right Resources Limited (www.right-resources.org.uk). She delivers a range of specialist training and support solutions to people and organizations.

details down or record them on your phone, this can help you feel more in control of what's coming next and help you feel less overwhelmed.

- Work out how best you can prepare yourself to cope. Be honest with yourself and reflect on the things you may be concerned about. Then think about what you could do to help deal with these.

- Find someone to talk to about your concerns and explore ways to cope with the challenges ahead.

It's Never Too Late

Delia Gascoigne, of Hampstead Dyslexia Clinic,* stresses that if you feel you need some extra support, go for it, no matter what stage of life you're in: 'While you are at school or college or even at work, it is never too late to seek additional help from dyslexia specialist tutors'.

In the experience of many in the book, help like this is so valuable. And there's other help available too, from teachers, YouTube, libraries, websites, local groups and more. Don't forget to seek out support wherever you can.

What Different Terms Mean

Dyslexia

According to the British Dyslexia Association:

* www.hampsteaddyslexiaclinic.co.uk

Dyslexia is a learning difficulty which primarily affects reading and writing skills. Dyslexic people may have difficulty processing and remembering information they see and hear, which can affect learning and the acquisition of literacy skills. Dyslexia can also impact on other areas such as organizational skills.

It is important to remember that there are positives to thinking differently. Many dyslexic people show strengths in areas such as reasoning and in visual and creative fields.*

Dysgraphia

Dysgraphia may mean impaired handwriting, impaired spelling (without reading problems), or both impaired handwriting and impaired spelling.

ADHD

Attention deficit hyperactivity disorder (ADHD) is described by the NHS as 'a condition that affects people's behaviour. People with ADHD can seem restless, may have trouble concentrating and may act on impulse.'** However, there are also benefits from having ADHD, with many saying it increases their energy levels, their ability to hyperfocus, their intuition, and more.

Dyspraxia

According to the Dyspraxia Foundation, this affects movement and balance. You may need extra effort in areas others find easy. Spatial awareness is poor. It can be

* www.bdadyslexia.org.uk

** www.nhs.uk/conditions/attention-deficit-hyperactivity-disorder-adhd

hard to learn new practical tasks. Organization may suffer and you may face difficulties with attention, memory, and time management. Many with dyspraxia describe positives that come with it, including problem-solving skills, the ability to multitask, and verbal dexterity.

Autism

The Autism Society says autism affects different people very differently. It can have an impact on social skills, communications, relationships, and self-regulation. You may have restricted behaviour or repeat the same behaviours over and again. There is no one cause. Many say autism also gives them great attention to detail, logical thinking, and pattern recognition skills, an ability to be goal orientated, and more.*

* See www.autismsociety.org for more information on autism

Further Reading

Dyslexia Is My Superpower (Most of the Time), by Margaret Rooke (JKP, 2017)

The Dyslexic Advantage: Unlocking the Hidden Potential of the Dyslexic Brain, by Dr Brock L. Eide and Dr Fernette F. Eide (Hay House, 2023)

Creative, Successful, Dyslexic: 23 High Achievers Share Their Stories, by Margaret Rooke (JKP, 2015)

School Spelling Dictionary, by Christine Maxwell and Julia Rowlandson (Barrington Stoke, 2012)

This Is Dyslexia, by Kate Griggs (Penguin, 2024)

The Power of Neurodiversity: Unleashing the Advantages of Your Differently Wired Brain, by Thomas Armstrong, PhD (Lifelong Books, 2011)

How to Talk So Teens Will Listen and Listen So Teens Will Talk, by Adele Faber and Elaine Mazlish (Piccadilly Press, 2012) (This one's for parents!)

Meet the Dyslexia Club, by Margaret Rooke (JKP, 2024) (This one's for younger kids!)

Further Help

School. Ask what help they can give. If you don't know this already, ask who in the school is in charge of Special Educational Needs.

Your national dyslexia organization, for instance the British Dyslexia Association, or Dyslexia Scotland, or Dyslexia Association Australia, or Dyslexia Ireland, or the International Dyslexia Association. They will have so much on their websites to help you.

Your community. Is there a local dyslexia group? Take a look online to check.

Instagram/TikTok/Facebook. Can you find a supportive group to help people in your area, such as Dyslexia Victoria Support (in Australia) or Dyslexia Support – for Parents of Dyslexic Children (worldwide)?

Others at your school – are there others with dyslexia you can talk to?

Acknowledgements

Thanks especially to everyone whose voices are included in this book, most of whom I first spoke to nearly ten years ago for *Dyslexia Is My Superpower (Most of the Time)*. Congratulations on being true to yourselves and taking your own paths. Wishing you all well in the years ahead.

Thanks to everyone at Jessica Kingsley Publishers. Special thanks to Amy Lankester-Owen, the editorial team, sales and marketing, the production team, and everyone else who makes the ship sail so successfully.

Big thanks to everyone who has listened to my thoughts about this book for many months (sorry!). Thanks to my lovely family and friends, and to my inspiring agent, Jane Judd.

Special thanks to Hannah for giving me the idea to write this.

With Thanks To

Anne Metcalfe
Barbara Reissner
Charles Freeman
City and Islington College, especially Matt Wojtyniak and Clive Ansell
DRC Generations, especially Isabel Dunsmuir
Dyslexia Coventry, especially Sarah Grainger
Dyslexia Ireland
Dyslexia Nigeria
Dyslexia Scotland, especially Katie Carmichael and Sue Bowen
Elizabeth Takyi
Hampstead Dyslexia Clinic, especially Delia Gascoigne
Heidi Gregory
Helen Arkell, especially Claire Harvey and Hazel Radnor
Janette Beetham
Lois Hood
Marcia Brissett-Bailey
Sarah Drummond
Tahirah Y. Yasin
The Amazing Dyslexics – Kathy Forsyth and Kate Power
The Dyslexic Advantage
Tomorrow's Generation
Waltham Forest Dyslexia Association

RAISING READERS

Books Build Bright Futures

Dear Reader,

We'd love your attention for one more page to tell you about the crisis in children's reading, and what we can all do.

Studies have shown that reading for fun is the **single biggest predictor of a child's future life chances** – more than family circumstance, parents' educational background or income. It improves academic results, mental health, wealth, communication skills, ambition and happiness.[1]

The number of children reading for fun is in rapid decline. Young people have a lot of competition for their time. In 2024, 1 in 10 children and young people in the UK aged 5 to 18 did not own a single book at home.[2]

Hachette works extensively with schools, libraries and literacy charities, but here are some ways we can all raise more readers:

- Reading to children for just 10 minutes a day makes a difference
- Don't give up if children aren't regular readers – there will be books for them!
- Visit bookshops and libraries to get recommendations
- Encourage them to listen to audiobooks
- Support school libraries
- Give books as gifts

There's a lot more information about how to encourage children to read on our website: **www.RaisingReaders.co.uk**

Thank you for reading.

hachette UK

1 OECD, '21st-Century Readers: Developing Literacy Skills in a Digital World', 2021, https://www.oecd.org/en/publications/21st-century-readers_a83d84cb-en.html

2 National Literacy Trust, 'Book Ownership in 2024', November 2024, https://literacytrust.org.uk/research-services/research-reports/book-ownership-in-2024